Treasuring Your Unborn Child

Composing A Legacy of Love for Your Unborn Child

My Baby's Name(s): ____________________

Our Pregnancy Dates: _____________ to _______________

Disclaimer

All information in this book is intended for educational and informational purposes only. The reader should consult with qualified medical, psychological, emotional, and spiritual professionals for treatment and help where needed. The narrated portions of this book were produced using AI generated voices from www.ElevenLabs.io.

Find more resources to treasure God, yourself, and your family at:

https://transforminglifepress.com

Publication Date: December 12, 2025. The Feast of Our Lady of Guadalupe, in the Jubilee Year of Hope

ISBN: 978-1-963227-59-8

Other books in the *Treasuring Your Unborn Child* series:

A Concert from Mary and Joseph to Expecting Dads
A Retreat with Mary and Joseph for Expecting Dads
Singing Treasuring Songs to Your Unborn Child, Expecting Moms Edition
Mary's Love Songs to Expecting Moms

This book is published by Transforming Life Press LLC, Poinciana, FL USA through Amazon KDP. Visit www.transforminglifepress.com for more titles.

Also by Dave Pipitone, *The Rainbow Chronicles: A Story of Hope for Today, Jubilee Year Edition* (Available on Amazon.com)

Date: ______________

My Gifting Letter to You

Table of Contents

Carry the Woman Who Carries Your Baby

Thank you for purchasing this book, *Composing a Legacy of Love for Your Unborn Child.* By using the information in this book, you can carry your wife (partner) and your unborn baby with God's love coming to them through you during pregnancy and childbirth.

There are five major sections of this book. Here is how to use them during this sacred time of God's creation. (Page 51 contains a more detailed description.)

A Concert from Mary and St. Joseph
Our Blessed Mother Mary and St. Joseph carry you in their prayers every moment to teach you the meaning of fatherhood. Listen to these contemporary Christian songs created just for you and your family. Listen to the Song Reflections deeper meaning. Let these compositions strike the chord of Mary and Joseph's love for you.

Composing a Legacy of Love
Before carrying anyone, you lift them up. This section sets the melody for you to carry the day for your baby's mental, emotional, and spiritual needs. Learn how to treasure your family here.

Treasuring Prayers
Let God's love carry you away, so your love can carry your family. God is creating your unborn child, just like God created you and your partner in your mothers' wombs. Learn how to do that here.

Treasuring Words
The thoughts and words you carry will create peace or stress, balance or uneasiness. Use this section to create a vocabulary and a strategy that keep your partner and baby safe and loved.

Treasuring Songs
God sings to all creation and we sing along. If you can't carry a tune, no worries! This section has you covered. There are 29 songs you can sing to your unborn child. Each song page has one or more QR Codes that takes you to a recorded version of the song. Just sing along.

Weekly Treasuring Action Pages
How do you carry out your love each week? Here's a practical, week-by-week guide. Create an action plan for each week to show your love and support. Watch a Weekly video with a QR code.

Get started with the next section, *A Concert by Mary and St. Joseph.* Just like Mary and St. Joseph were the parents of Jesus, they are your spiritual parents. Their presence, prayers, support and love are with you every day.

A Concert from Mary and St. Joseph

Carried by Mary and St. Joseph

You are a son to Mary and St. Joseph, your spiritual parents who carry you in their prayers. They cooperated with God to bring Jesus into the world through Mary's pregnancy and childbirth. Mary and Joseph have loved you since your conception. Now, they are sending their love to you, your partner, and unborn child.

Many men do not experience the deep spiritual love of God through their natural parents. Without that love, it is easy to lack support as a father in their lives. When Mary and Joseph formed the Holy Family, they showed their devotion to each other and their unborn child, Jesus. Now in Heaven, Mary and Joseph's care are with you in a graced way with their prayers and presence.

Jesus entrusted Mary to be the mother of all His followers. He gave her to His beloved disciple as He was dying on the Cross. St. Joseph was the earthly father of Jesus. He took a pregnant Mary into his home, cared for her, protected his family, and raised Jesus.

This section contains 16 songs to imagine the love that Mary and Joseph have for you. Their love carries you through your entire life, and especially now during your pregnancy. These songs help you visualize how Mary and St. Joseph teach you to be a good husband, father, and man. Listen to them, not society's view.

The songs' lyrics and melodies were composed and produced by Emma Bennett and her talented team. Emma is an inspired Christian Gospel singer from London, United Kingdom. The songs include solos and duets, imagining the voices of Mary and Joseph, as they sing to you and each other.

The song themes include Mary and Joseph's love and parenting for you. Their messages honor God and encourage you to become a man of virtue, gentle yet strong. They invite you to obey God the Father, believe in Jesus, and listen to the Holy Spirit. Two 'bonus' songs visualize songs to celebrate their marriage and the day of Jesus' birth. Listen with your partner too.

Each song has two pages. The first page contains the title of the song, the reason for the song, the lyrics, and a QR code for each track. Scan the QR code with your mobile device, and tap on the SoundCloud link to play the song. Listen to the song with your wife and unborn child.

The second page offers a reflection on the song's lyrics and meaning for your time as an expecting dad. My AI friend, Jerry B, narrates these reflections. Scan the QR code to listen to the reflection as you read along.

We Love You, Our Son

Stirring Duet   Gentle Duet

Why This Song?

This song imagines the love that Mary and Joseph have for you as their spiritual child and their encouragement on the journey to fatherhood.

Lyrics

We've watched you from the silence
As you stumbled through your days
So many questions in your heart
And love that has no place
But heaven sees you clearly,
And I've whispered in your ear
You're not alone, my son
My heart is always near

I know the weight you're carrying
I bore it in my time
Uncertain hands, a trembling voice
Yet chosen by design
God doesn't ask for perfect men
But those who dare to stay
And in your "yes," my son
You lead the narrow way

We love you, our son
With a love that won't fade
In your quiet battles
In the promise you've made
When the world feels heavy
When the road feels long
We're standing beside you
You are brave, you are strong.
You are loved… You belong…

You'll hold a child against your chest
And feel your soul ignite
Your fear will kneel before your love
And morning follows night
Let every moment draw you in
To grace beyond your past
You are not who the world defined
You're chosen first, not last

Let heaven shape your fatherhood
Like it shaped mine through trust
And when you fall, I'll lift you up
Like I once held Jesus
You're not just a father
You are a son, too
A beloved, called, and cherished son
Of the Father true

We love you, our son
With a love that won't fade
In your quiet battles
In the promise you've made
When the night feels endless.
And the answers are few
We are praying for you
God is working through you.
You are loved… You belong…
You are strong… You are son

We Love You, Our Son

Reflection

The song, *We Love You, Our Son*, offers you insights into the love that Mary and Joseph have for you–as their spiritual son. Every person has natural parents, a mother and a father who cooperated with God to bring a new life into being. Every person has a Heavenly Father, our Creator, who made us out of nothing. And, because of God's action in human history to send His Son Jesus to become a human being, Jesus' parents are our parents.

Song Insights

What are some of the ways that Mary and Joseph show their love to you? Look at the chorus of this song:

*We love you, our son, with a love that won't fade, in your quiet battles in the promise you've made. When the world feels heavy, when the road feels long, we're standing beside you. You are brave, you are strong. You are loved… You belong…*Good parents seek the best for their children, sacrifice for their health, and well-being.

Let heaven shape your fatherhood, like it shaped mine through trust. And when you fall, I'll lift you up like I once held Jesus. You're not just a father, you are a son, too. a beloved, called, and cherished son Of the Father true.

On a spiritual level, Mary and Joseph are 'in your corner' for you and your loved ones. Because they are the parents of Jesus, Mary and Joseph have a direct 'hot line' to their Son to ask for favors and blessings.

An Invitation to Listen

As you listen to this song, there are two renditions, each one sung as a duet. The first rendition is stirring - with a lively tempo and joyful vocals. The second rendition has a gentle instrumental and softer vocals.

Listen to the rendition that most resonates with your mood. Ask your spouse to listen with you. Allow your unborn child to hear the music with you. Mary and Joseph are the spiritual parents to everyone in your family. The more you hear this song, the greater your faith in Mary and Joseph's love will become.

Stirring

Duet

Tender

Duet

Always in Your Heart

Why This Song?

This song imagines the presence of Mary and Joseph with you and your family, always close to you in your heart.

Lyrics

You may not see us standing
But we've never stepped away
The journey feels like yours alone
But we walk with you each day

When the weight begins to tremble
In the silence of the night
Know that I have prayed beside you
With my hands upon your life
You may not hear my whisper
But my love is always near
You are never just one man…
You are one we hold dear

We are always in your heart
Even when you feel apart
When you doubt the strength you carry
And the road feels long and hard…
You are not alone, dear son
You are cradled in our prayers
We are always, always in your heart

I've stood where you are standing
With questions I could not speak
But strength was in the stillness
And God's peace was in the weak
You might not feel our footsteps
But I promise you, they're there
Every moment that you love her
Is a moment we are near

We are always in your heart
Not just when you kneel and pray
But in your quiet, sacred choices
That shape your child each day
We are not far away from you
Our love will not depart
We are always, always in your heart

When fear begins to whisper…
When strength feels out of reach…
Let love be what surrounds you
Let grace be what you teach

The Father hears you deeply…
And we are interceding still
You are a vessel of His promise
Chosen for His will

So carry on in courage
Though your knees may
Shake and bend
For every "yes" you offer
Helps God's story never end
Your child will see your heartbeat
And in time will understand:
That love is more than presence…
It's a prayer that holds their hand

We are always in your heart
Like the stars that guard the night
In your joy and in your silence
We are holding you in light
You were never meant to walk alone
He's been with you from the start
And so have we…
Always in your heart

Always in Your Heart

Reflection

The song, *Always in Your Heart*, offers you insights into the presence that Mary and Joseph have in your life. They are always there–in times of joy and sorrow, in times of need and plenty. As our spiritual mother and father, now living in Heaven, we can't see them physically. Yet our faith holds the hope of their watchful care over the small and large details of our lives.

Song Insights

What are some of the ways that Mary and Joseph show their care for you and your family? The song lyrics offer these insights: 1) you are held dear; 2) they are with you when the 'road feels long and hard' 3) their lives on earth had challenges, joys, and sorrows like yours; 4) they are present when you love your wife and unborn baby; 5) they applaud the 'yes' you say to holding your child's hand.

Think about this the words in this verse:

We are always in your heart, not just when you kneel and pray, but in your quiet, sacred choices that shape your child each day. We are not far away from you; our love will not depart. We are always, always in your heart.

On a spiritual level, Mary and Joseph are always available to you and your loved ones. Because they are the parents of Jesus, their prayers are heard and answered for favors and blessings.

An Invitation to Listen

As you listen to this song, there are two renditions, each one sung as a duet. The first rendition is stirring - with a lively tempo and joyful vocals. The second rendition offers tender vocals and softer instrumentals.

Listen to the rendition that most resonates with your mood. Ask your spouse to listen with you. Allow your unborn child to hear the music with you. Mary and Joseph are the spiritual parents to everyone in your family. The more you hear this song, the greater your faith in Mary and Joseph's presence in your heart.

God's Dream for You

Mellow Duet

Folk Mary

Why This Song?

This song recalls Joseph's dreams that God led him and will lead you to love and support your family.

Lyrics

In this season, you feel the weight
A future unfolding
A love that won't wait
Like Joseph in the night
With dreams sent from above,
God whispers in your heart
"This child will be love."

So hold on, dear father
To the dreams He's sown
With faith as your anchor
You're never alone
Through the trials and the joys
In every tear and smile
God's dream for you is shining
Guiding you each mile

When doubts start lurking
And shadows draw near
Remember Joseph's journey
Let go of your fear
For the angels are singing
A message clear and bright
"Fear not, for He is with you
Through the darkest night."

So hold on, dear father
To the dreams He's sown
With faith as your anchor
You're never alone
Through the trials and the joys
In every tear and smile
God's dream for you is shining
Through every trial

In the stillness of the night
As you cradle your child
Know that every heartbeat
Reflects love so mild
With each step you take
May His wisdom unfold
You're a part of His story
A journey untold

And when the road is winding
And the path feels unclear
Trust in the promise
God's presence is near
For every dream you nurture
Every prayer that you share
Is a piece of His kingdom,
A testament of care

So hold on, dear father
To the dreams He's sown
With faith, love, and hope
You're never alone
Through the trials and the joys
In every tear and smile
God's dream for you is shining
Guiding all the while

God's Dream for You

Reflection

The song, *God's Dream for You*, offers you insights into the gift of dreams. The Gospel of Matthew told how God communicated to Joseph through dreams of an angel's speech. The angel directed Joseph to honor Mary, accept the child she was carrying, and protect their family.

God is always talking with you, directly, through other people and events to lead you as a father to honor and protect your family. God will speak to you through your dreams, too.

Song Insights

Your family's pregnancy is a journey with a beginning, and end, and an uncertain middle. There is a regular pattern of your child's physical development and growth. God is present the entire time to your family, speaking to you, your wife, and your unborn child.

This song encourages repeatedly. Take a look at this chorus:

So hold on, dear father to the dreams He's sown, with faith as your anchor you're never alone. Through the trials and the joys, in every tear and smile, God's dream for you is shining, guiding you each mile.

Trust that God cares for you during this journey of pregnancy, and every moment of life.

An Invitation to Listen

As you listen to this song, there are two renditions, each one sung as a duet. The first rendition is mellow - with a relaxed tempo and joyful vocals. The second rendition offers tender vocals and a folk instrumental.

Listen to the rendition that most resonates with your mood. Ask your spouse to listen with you. Allow your unborn child to hear the music with you. Mary and Joseph are the spiritual parents to everyone in your family. The more you hear this song, the greater your faith that God is speaking to you about His dream for your family.

Obey the Father

Stirring	Lively	Stirring
Duet	Mary	Mary

Why This Song?

This song imagines the faithfulness of Joseph and Mary as God called them through angels and dreams to love their family.

Lyrics

He didn't give me every answer
But He gave me His voice
And that was enough…
To make the right choice

I had dreams of comfort
Plans that felt like mine
Then He broke the silence
With a calling so divine
It didn't make much sense then
But peace grew with each "yes."
Obedience is not the easy road
But it is always blessed

Obey the Father, even when it's hard
Even when your heart is trembling
Even when you're in the dark
It's not about perfection
It's about where you stand
You build your house on Heaven
When you follow His command

I led her through the desert
With nothing but His Word
Each step we took in silence
Still somehow reassured
And every time I doubted
He whispered back to me
"I am the One who called you
I am all you need to see."

Obey the Father
Even through the storm
Even when the journey breaks you
He will carry you with form
You are not alone, son
He walks with you every land
You are shaping holy ground
When you follow His command

You may never get applause
You may never feel prepared…
But legacy begins
With the love that's dared to care

This child will watch you closely
Learn from what you do
So let your choices echo
What the Father speaks to you
No crown will ever matter
No wealth can understand
The glory of a man who says
"Yes, Lord… here I am."

Obey the Father…
Even when it's small
For every act of courage
Can change it all
You're not just raising children
You're answering His plan…
Obey the Father
Be the righteous man

Obey the Father

Reflection

God the Father is the Source of all love and life, Who directs all creation according to His Will and Plan for good. God's wisdom is beyond any human thought or reasoning. The Father created all human beings with free will. We can choose to follow the Father's wisdom or not. When we choose to obey the Father's laws, guidance, commandments, we invite a life of joy and happiness for ourselves and others. When we choose a selfish way, we make life miserable. Choose to Obey the Father.

Song Insights

The words in the verses of this song share the struggle to do what we want and to do what God wants. *Obey the Father, even when it's hard. Obey the Father, even through the storm. Obey the Father, even when it's small.*

This child will watch you closely, learn from what you do, so let your choices echo, what the Father speaks to you. No crown will ever matter, no wealth can understand the glory of a man who says "Yes, Lord… here I am."
Your child will be watching you and learning from you, even now in your wife's womb.

Obey the Father…even when it's small, for every act of courage can change it all. You're not just raising children, you're answering His plan… Obey the Father, be the righteous man. Like Joseph, you can become the righteous man for your family.

An Invitation to Listen

As you listen to this song, there are three renditions, one sung as a duet and two as 'Mary' female solos. The first and third renditions are stirring - with an upbeat tempo and joyful vocals. The second rendition offers lively vocals with a matching instrumental.

Listen to the rendition that most resonates with your mood. Ask your spouse to listen with you. Allow your unborn child to hear the music with you. Mary and Joseph are the spiritual parents to everyone in your family. The more you hear this song, the greater your willingness to participate in God the Father's plan for you and your family.

Lively Duet — Stirring Duet

Believe in Jesus

Why This Song?

This song is a duet of Mary and Joseph calling and inviting you to believe in their Son Jesus and His love for your family.

Lyrics

Before He walked on water
Before He calmed the sea
He lived within our shelter
And trusted you and me

I said yes with trembling hands
Not knowing what would come
But deep inside, I heard His voice
And carried God's own Son
He grew beneath my heartbeat
As I learned to walk by grace
And every time I feared the dark
He lit my soul with faith

I almost turned away in fear
But still I chose to stay
For when an angel spoke to me
I bowed my plans and prayed
I didn't fully understand
But still I made a place
To guard the Light of all the world
With strength and quiet faith

Believe in Jesus
Even when you cannot see
He's in the cries, the kicks, the silence
He is in your family
What feels small is sacred
What feels hidden still is true
He is growing in your story
And He's working now through you

They didn't see the glory
Just a mother, just a girl
But heaven knew the story
Would one day change the world
So trust what's born in silence
Even if it comes with pain
For every act of love you give
Will not be done in vain

You don't need to be a prophet
Just a man who stays and prays
Who lifts the weight, who lights the fire
Who leads with patient grace
It's not the world that crowns you
It's not applause that shows
It's obedience in the shadows
That only Heaven knows

Believe in Jesus
When the road is hard to hold
When the future feels uncertain
Still your love can make Him known
Every breath, each sleepless night
Each moment you defend
You're protecting someone holy
Who lives beyond the world's end

He is life within your waiting
He is peace in every storm
He's the voice inside your fatherhood
The truth you will transform
He is with you… He is in you…
He is the reason you believe

So rise with quiet courage
And live the way we did
Give your heart to what is growing
To the dreams you'll one day lift
For the child in your keeping
Is part of Heaven's plan
So believe in Jesus
And be a faithful man

Believe in Jesus…
He's closer than you know
He trusted you to carry Him
Now let that mercy grow

Believe in Jesus

Reflection

The Father sent His Son Jesus, to redeem us from our selfish ways and show us His Father's face. Jesus always obeyed the Father. Jesus died on the Cross to destroy sin and His Father raised Jesus from the dead to new life.

When we believe in Jesus, and follow Him, we participate in that new life for ourselves and other people. Choose to Believe in Jesus.

Song Insights

This song stirs your heart and imagination to visualize how Mary and Joseph believed in Jesus, while He was an unborn child, after birth, and during their encounter with Him during their earthly lives. Now, they live with Jesus forever in Heaven.

Believe in Jesus, even when you can't see, He's in the cries, the kicks, the silence, He's in your family. Jesus is there, hidden in the plain and simple.

Believe in Jesus, when the road is hard to hold, when the future feels uncertain still your love can make Him known. There will be times when you feel 'up' and uncertain during your life. Keep believing.

Believe in Jesus… He's closer than you know, He trusted you to carry Him, now let that mercy grow. Jesus helps you to let your baby grow.

An Invitation to Listen

As you listen to this song, there are two renditions, both sung as a duet. The first rendition is lively - with an upbeat tempo and joyful vocals. The second rendition offers stirring vocals with a matching instrumental.

Listen to the rendition that most resonates with your mood. Ask your spouse to listen with you. Allow your unborn child to hear the music with you. Mary and Joseph are the spiritual parents to everyone in your family. The more you hear this song, the more you can realize how believing in Jesus, like Mary and Joseph did, will bring you more peace and love during your pregnancy.

Lively Mary

Stirring Mary

Listen to the Holy Spirit

Why This Song?

This song invites you to recognize and act on the whispering of the Holy Spirit during your daily living and pregnancy journey.

Lyrics

There's a voice you won't hear loudly
But it whispers in your bones.
He speaks between your questions…
Beyond all you'll ever own

You watch her belly rising
Not sure what you should do
But beneath the skin and silence
The Spirit speaks to you
The same One who shaped the oceans
Now stirs the child unseen…
And He whispers in your knowing
Through every cell and gene

Listen to the Holy Spirit
He's nearer than your breath
He's weaving songs of mercy
In the stillness you have left
Not every step will thunder
Not every sign will glow…
But if you lean into His whisper
He will teach you what to know

He hovers over water still
Like in the days of birth
Creating from the formless dust
A soul that shakes the earth
So hold this moment gently
Let silence be your part
For the Spirit who made galaxies
Now speaks within your heart

Listen to the Holy Spirit
He speaks in gentle ways
In your patience, in your loving
In the prayers you barely say
You don't need to know the ending
You don't need a burning sign
Just trust the quiet shaping
Of the Spirit over time

He sings to your unborn child
Songs not meant for ears
He shapes her spine with silence
And soothes his tiny fears
So, when you rest your hands on her
And bless that sacred place…
You're joining in creation
Through the Spirit's voice of grace

So tune your ears to wonder
Don't rush the sacred bloom
For growth begins in stillness
Like a flower finds its room
Let Him guide your footsteps
As you guard this holy flame
He knows your child already…
And He gently speaks your name

Listen to the Holy Spirit…
There's no need to fear or strive
He is writing something eternal
In the rhythm of this life
So be still, be brave, be open
For the whisper is your part…
And the One who forms the cosmos
Is speaking… to your heart

Listen to the Holy Spirit

Reflection

Jesus promised those who believe in Him, that He would send the Holy Spirit to them as a guide, comforter, and advocate. The Holy Spirit would give spiritual power and life to those who believe in Jesus and follow Him.

The Holy Spirit gives spiritual gifts and reminds us of Jesus' words. At the Catholic Mass, the priest asks the Father to send the Holy Spirit to consecrate the bread and wine to become the Body and Blood of Jesus. Choose to listen to the Holy Spirit.

Song Insights

This wonderful song illustrates several ways the Holy Spirit 'breathes' new life in your pregnancy.

But beneath the skin and silence, the Spirit speaks to you, the same One who shaped the oceans now stirs the child unseen… The Holy Spirit is involved with the creation of your baby, just as when He shaped the oceans.

He sings to your unborn child, songs not meant for ears, He shapes her spine with silence and soothes his tiny fears. The Holy Spirit is at work shaping your child during its time in the womb.

And the One who forms the cosmos is speaking… to your heart. The Holy Spirit reaches inside you to whisper His love and guidance. Listen!

An Invitation to Listen

As you listen to this song, there are two renditions, both sung as a 'Mary' female solo. The first rendition is lively - with an upbeat tempo and joyful vocals. The second rendition offers stirring vocals with a matching instrumental.

Listen to the rendition that most resonates with your mood. Ask your spouse to listen with you. Allow your unborn child to hear the music with you. Mary and Joseph are the spiritual parents to everyone in your family. The more you hear this song, the more you can learn to trust that the Holy Spirit speaks to you every day.

Gentle

Mary

Tender

Mary

A Man of God

Why This Song?

This song imagines the admiration that Mary has for Joseph and his devotion to God, which supported and protected her and unborn Jesus.

Lyrics

Joseph, my dear, this song is for you – and all the men you will inspire by your love for our family – and all families to come…

I carried Heaven's promise,
But I was still a girl
And in that sacred silence
You stood and chose the world

You said no words of anger,
Though you could have walked away.
You let love guide your trembling hands,
And faith became your stay.
In the hush between my heartbeats,
In the dark no one could see
You gave your "yes" beside me
And built a home for me

You are a man of God
Not just in what you say
But in how you stayed
In how you prayed
In how you made a way
Not crowned with gold or thunder
But with mercy wide and broad
I raised the Son of Heaven
But you showed me a man of God

Each night you lit the lantern
And watched me fall asleep
You dreamed with open eyes
And promises you'd keep

I saw the fear you never voiced,
The weight that pressed you low
But you carried it with dignity
And taught our Son to grow

You are a man of God
Steady in the storm
With calloused hands
You held His plan
And kept His promise warm
Not with loud, triumphant wonders
But with every quiet nod
I bore the Christ of Glory
But you lived as a man of God

There's no halo in the silence,
No spotlight in the night
Just a man who hears the whisper
And still chooses what is right.

[I was never just a mother,
And you were more than just a guide.
You were the doorway for the miracle,
The faith God placed beside

To every man who wonders
If he has what it takes
Remember Joseph's silence
And how Heaven knew his name
You are a man of God…
Yes, you are a man of God

A Man of God

Reflection

Joseph thought of dismissing his wife when he learned she was expecting a child, not from him. An angel spoke to Joseph in a dream to tell him about her future in raising a savior. Joseph listened and took Mary into his home, and raised Jesus with her. The Gospel of Matthew calls Joseph, a righteous man–a man who loved and obeyed God. Joseph was called "A Man of God."

Song Insights

You are called to be a man of God for your family, during your pregnancy and every day afterwards. What does that involve?

In the dark no one could see you gave your "yes" beside me and built a home for me. Just as Joseph built a home for Mary and Jesus, you say "yes" to your family, by building a safe place to live, love and honor them.

You are a man of God, not just in what you say but in how you stayed, in how you prayed, in how you made a way. Being a man of God for your family goes beyond just words, it's in the staying, the praying, and making a way.

You are a man of God, steady in the storm with calloused hands, you held His plan and kept His promise warm. Stay steady during the storms of life, like Joseph. Believe in God's plan and promise for your family.

An Invitation to Listen

As you listen to this song, there are two renditions, both sung as a 'Mary' female solo. The first rendition is gentle - with a soft tempo and joyful vocals. The second rendition offers tender vocals with a matching instrumental.

Listen to the rendition that most resonates with your mood. Ask your spouse to listen with you. Allow your unborn child to hear the music with you. Mary and Joseph are the spiritual parents to everyone in your family. The more you hear this song, the more you can model being a man of God for your family, like Joseph was for his family.

A Responsible Father

Stirring Mary   Folk Mary

Why This Song?

This song is sung by Hazel Charles, voicing the desire of Mary to dads who stand up to be the loving men and fathers they can be.

At every peaceful moment in the morning light
Rise before the world awakes
Look to do what's right
With steady hands and loving heart
Give more of your life as time imparts

Steer your family
Through storms and rains
Not just words
But act justly when in pain
Be a compass in the darkest night
Let your footsteps
Walk with courage bright

Here's to you, a steadfast guide
A lantern bright that never hides
Your love's a flame that never dies
A father in The Father's eyes
With joy and pains of doing right
Responsible through every sight
Your legacy will always show
A way for fatherhood to glow
A bond beyond compare
A father's love, a father's care

When doubts would whisper
Don't believe the lies
That steal your peace
And cloud the skies
With patient words and open arms
Keep your loved ones safe from harm
Teach them what love means
Be the father of their dreams

Here's to you, a steadfast guide
A lantern bright that never hides
Your love's a flame that never dies
A father in The Father's eyes.
With joy and pains of doing right
Responsible through every sight
Your legacy will always show
A way for fatherhood to glow
A bond beyond compare
A father's love, a father's care

Work hard to build your home
A place where hope can grow
Let their eyes see your strength
To make the world a place to glow
May your footsteps
Echo on through time
In every child you raise
May your kindness with each word said
In every path your family treads

Stand up now on grown-up ground
Carry what you gave
Let your wisdom whisper in their lives
The gift of how to brave
So here's my song of gratitude
A promise that we will keep
The love God has for you
Will make your heart leap

Be a man of honor in all you do
Let your love always be seen
A responsible father, strong and true
Make your wife your queen
More than a Bible text
Your legacy will rise
From one generation to next
Your heart's the greatest prize

A Responsible Father

Reflection

Being responsible involves making a response that honors the life situation you are encountering. As an expecting dad, you are a responsible father. That means you make positive decisions and take positive actions to honor your wife and children.

There are many circumstances in family life where you can seek only your good, and ignore what you can do for the good of your family. Love seeks to do the highest good of other people. Loving your family makes you a responsible father.

Song Insights

This song has many 'Proverbs' sayings that make up your journey as a responsible father:

Don't believe the lies, that steal your peace and cloud the skies

With patient words and open arms, keep your loved ones safe from harm

Teach them what love means, be the father of their dreams

Work hard to build your home a place where hope can grow

Let their eyes see your strength to make the world a place to glow

Be a man of honor in all you do, let your love always be seen

A responsible father, strong and true, make your wife your queen

Examine what you do and make it the best for your family.

An Invitation to Listen

As you listen to this song, there are two renditions, both sung as a 'Mary' female solo. The first rendition is stirring - with an upbeat tempo and joyful vocals. The second rendition offers country-style vocals with a matching folk music instrumental.

Listen to the rendition that most resonates with your mood. Ask your spouse to listen with you. Allow your unborn child to hear the music with you. Mary and Joseph are the spiritual parents to everyone in your family. The more you listen to this song, the more you can appreciate your role to become a responsible father like Joseph was for his family.

Gentle Duet | Stirring Duet

Gentle, Yet Strong

Why This Song?

This song imagines the gentle strength that Joseph used to guard, protect, and love his family during their journey of life.

Lyrics

They thought strength meant
Raising a fist
But God taught me to raise a cradle

The world saw a carpenter
But Heaven saw a shield
A man who'd hold the silence
And not demand to feel
I wasn't made for battles
At least not loud and wild
But to build a place of peace
For a woman and a child

Gentle, yet strong
Like rivers that shape stone
I learned that love holds longer
When it walks, not when it roars
Patient, not passive
Tender, but never gone
This is the strength I carry
Gentle… yet strong

She wept in midnight aching
I held her without words
The silence was a language
And faith was what we heard
I didn't know all answers
I just stayed through every turn
For sometimes love is choosing
Not to leave when others would've run

Gentle, yet strong
Like roots beneath the tree
I found my power not in force
But in quiet loyalty
Present, not perfect
Faithful all along
I walked beside her carrying
A strength… that made me strong.

God, You didn't ask for thunder
You just asked me to be near
You gave me hands to guide
Not fists to rule in fear

Now every man who wonders
If quiet love is brave
Let him look at how You came to us
In a manger, not a blade

Strength is not in shouting…
It's in staying all night long
May God make you like He made me
Gentle… yet strong

Gentle, Yet Strong

Reflection

What do you think makes a man and father strong? Strong muscles? Strong finances? Strong reputation? Ability to win a fist fight?

What do you believe about being gentle? Is it a sign of weakness? A sign of being a doormat? A sign of failure?

As a carpenter, Joseph was a strong man to use tools and physical effort to work, shape and build with wood. Yet, as the earthly father to Jesus, Joseph cared for his boy when he was tiny, and as Jesus grew. Joseph was gentle, yet strong. And so can you be.

Song Insights

What does gentle, yet strong look like? Consider these lyrics:

Patient, not passive, tender, but never gone; this is the strength I carry, gentle… yet strong. Being a father means staying, being patient and tender.

I didn't know all answers, I just stayed through every turn, for sometimes love is choosing not to leave when others would've run. You may not know all the answers, but you can serve your family, and not leave.

Gentle, yet strong, like roots beneath the tree, I found my power not in force, but in quiet loyalty. A tree falls over without deep roots, which no one sees. The same is true of your quiet loyalty.

Present, not perfect, faithful all along I walked beside her carrying a strength… that made me strong. Be a faithful father, be there, it will make you strong.

An Invitation to Listen

As you listen to this song, there are two renditions, both sung as a duet. The first rendition is like the song title - gentle, yet strong - with a soft tempo and joyful vocals. The second rendition offers stirring vocals with a matching instrumental.

Listen to the rendition that most resonates with your mood. Ask your spouse to listen with you. Allow your unborn child to hear the music with you. Mary and Joseph are the spiritual parents to everyone in your family. The more you hear this song, the better you can model gentleness and patience during your pregnancy.

The Wonder of Your Child

Gentle Mary   Tender Mary

Why This Song?

This song imagines Mary singing of the wonder of your child, just like carrying and raising her child Jesus was a time of wonder for her.

Lyrics

I once held the face of God
Before He spoke a word
And in that fragile silence
My whole world turned.

There's a wonder in the waiting,
A holiness in pain
There's beauty in becoming
When nothing feels the same
I didn't choose the pathway
But I said "yes" in fear and grace
And from that trembling whisper
God gave the world His face

The wonder of your child
Will unfold in days to come
You'll hear heaven in the laughter
And hold mercy by the thumb
You are being changed forever
Your child's soul begins to rise
Don't miss the sacred moments
A miracle of life before your eyes

I watched Him chase the butterflies,
And cry when He was scared.
I held Him close at midnight
When no one else had cared.
Don't search for signs and thunder
It's little things your child will do
Every heartbeat you carry
Is God's promise made through you

The wonder of your child
Is not just flesh and breath
But are eternity in motion
A whisper out of death
And in your love, a blossom
Like the stars that kiss the skies
You are raising someone holy,
With a spark of paradise.

She may not walk on water
Or wear a crown of flame
But don't you dare forget, my son
Each child is called by name
And if you choose to love him
To guard her day and night
Then through your heart
God's light will shine so bright

So hold him with your patience
And let your kindness lead
She does not need perfection
He only needs your peace
You are more than just a father
You are chosen to reveal
The wonder of a story
That only love can seal

The wonder of your child…
Will teach you how to see
That every life, no matter small
Holds echoes of the King
So cherish her, protect him
Let your love be undefiled…
You are walking with a Savior…
In the wonder of your child

The Wonder of Your Child

Reflection

Have you ever seen a miracle? Go into your bathroom and look in the mirror. Every human being is made of wonder, carries wonder, and is wonder full. Every person in your family is made of wonder, a living miracle.

Jesus was a Child of wonder, that Mary conceived, gave birth to, and raised. So, too, your unborn child is a child of wonder. A beautiful person who is living and growing now. Only God knows how your child's life will unfold–and it will be full of wonder.

Song Insights

What are some images of wonder from this song's lyrics that honor the miracle of your unborn child? Consider these:

The wonder of your child will unfold in days to come; you'll hear heaven in the laughter and hold mercy by the thumb. Imagine the echo of God's pleasure in your child's laugh, and you holding that mercy by your child's thumb.

And in your love, a blossom like the stars that kiss the skies, you are raising someone holy, with a spark of paradise. Your child is holy, destined for a life in paradise, in Heaven, with you and God forever.

An Invitation to Listen

As you listen to this song, there are two renditions, both sung as a 'Mary' female solo. The first rendition is gentle - with a soft tempo and joyful vocals. The second rendition offers tender vocals with a matching instrumental.

Listen to the rendition that most resonates with your mood. Ask your spouse to listen with you. Allow your unborn child to hear the music with you. Mary and Joseph are the spiritual parents to everyone in your family. The more you listen to this song, the more you can honor the wonder of life in you, your partner, and your unborn child.

Stirring Duet

Tender Mary

Wondrously Made

Why This Song?

This song recalls the promise of Psalm 139, and how God made you in a wonderful way, just like He is creating your unborn child.

Lyrics

Who are we, that You are mindful of us?
Yet You formed us in the secret place
And called us good

Before she felt the flutter
Before the world could know
God whispered life inside her womb
A masterpiece to grow
But not just child or mother
You too are shaped divine
A father formed with heaven's breath
God's image intertwined

You are wondrously made
Fearfully, joyfully born
Knitted in mystery, held by His gaze
Before the dawn at morn
From mother to child
From heartbeat to hands
Every life is a canvas
Of the great "I Am."

I once felt unworthy
A man of wood and dust
But God does not create mistakes
He builds men He can trust
I saw the sacred in her tears
And felt it in her womb
Not just the child was being made
But the father was made too

You are wondrously made
In silence and in light
Every scar and sleepless night
Still precious in His sight
From soul to soul
Through joy and ache
Every life is a miracle
God chose to wake

You knit me in the secret place…
What is man
That You are mindful of him?
I praise You
For I am fearfully made…
Crowned with glory, formed in Him

So if you ever wonder
When your joy turns into strife
Remember Who has made you
And called you into life
You're not just here to witness
You're part of Heaven's thread
A father, mother, child of God
All wondrously made

Wondrously made…
And wonderfully loved
A family formed by grace
A gift from above

Wondrously Made

Reflection

God doesn't make junk. Every gift of creation carries a mark of its Creator. Whether that gift is a flower, a mountain, a field of grain, or an unborn child, all is wondrously made. Yet, even more so for human beings, made in God's Divine image and likeness.

In Psalm 139, the writer asks who are human beings, so tiny when compared to the vastness of the universe? We are wondrously made by a wonder full God.

Song Insights

Focus on the lyrics and lines that speak of how you, your spouse, and your baby are wondrously made:

But not just child or mother, you too are shaped divine, a father formed with heaven's breath, God's image intertwined. As a father, God is shaping you with the image of the Father, to share with your family.

I once felt unworthy, a man of wood and dust, but God does not create mistakes, He builds men He can trust. God is trusting you with your unborn child. Your baby is no mistake and neither are you. God wants both of you to live with Him forever.

I saw the sacred in her tears, and felt it in her womb, not just the child was being made, but the father was made too. Your child is sacred, and you are being made into a father during this pregnancy, too.

An Invitation to Listen

As you listen to this song, there are two renditions, one sung as a duet and the other sung as a 'Mary' female solo. The first rendition is a stirring duet - with a dynamic tempo and moving vocals. The second rendition offers tender vocals with a matching instrumental.

Listen to the rendition that most resonates with your mood. Ask your spouse to listen with you. Allow your unborn child to hear the music with you. Mary and Joseph are the spiritual parents to everyone in your family. The more you hear this song, the more you can experience how sacred you and your family are to God.

The Thoughts You Have for Me

Mellow Duet | Folk Duet

Why This Song?

This song is about a future full of hope, peace and prosperity in your family, based on Jeremiah 29:11

Lyrics

In this moment, I feel Your guiding hand
Gently leading my steps
Through this weary land
Though the path seems unclear
My vision's blurred
I trust the future promised in Your Word

For I know the thoughts You have for me
Plans to prosper, hope and family
A future filled with love's warm embrace
As I follow after Your amazing grace

My beloved walks beside me on this road
Sharing life's journey
Lightening every load
Together we'll rise
To meet the days ahead
Sheltered by the promises
Your voice has said

For I know the thoughts You have for me
Plans to prosper, hope and family
A future filled with love's warm embrace
As I follow after Your amazing grace

When doubts and fears arise
To cloud my view
I'll fix my eyes on the One
Who makes all things new
In faith I'll carry on without dismay
Walking in the visions You've cast my way

Through seasons of rain and radiant sun
We'll weather each storm
As two become one
Hand in hand we'll climb
Toward that distant shore
Where joy everlasting
Will reign forever more

For I know the thoughts You have for me
Plans to prosper, hope and family
A future filled with love's warm embrace
As I follow after Your amazing grace

In this quiet moment, my heart overflows
With thankful praise
For the love heaven bestows
The gift of your presence
To cherish and keep
A blessed assurance
That gently puts my soul to sleep

For I know the thoughts You have for me
Plans to prosper, hope and family
A future filled with love's warm embrace
As I follow after Your amazing grace

You shared your plans
In wondrous dreams
To show this life is more than it seems
Your amazing grace leads my way
My God, my all, with You I will stay

The Thoughts You Have for Me

Reflection

What does God think about you? About this pregnancy? About the meaning of your life? God thinks a lot about you. In fact, God has a plan for you–a plan to prosper you and give you a future of hope. And more than that–God has those same thoughts for your family, too.

When doubts arise and other thoughts try to steal your peace, listen to God's thoughts for you. Pick up the Bible. Read about God's promises to you. Focus on what God says to you, not others who attempt to discourage, dishonor, or discredit you. God's thoughts are beyond all human doubts, fears or worries.

Song Insights

Consider the chorus from the song:

For I know the thoughts You have for me
Plans to prosper, hope and family
A future filled with love's warm embrace
As I follow after Your amazing grace

God's amazing grace leads your way, a loving warm embrace, plans for hope, family, and all the good things God has in store for you–in this life and in the life to come in Heaven.

An Invitation to Listen

As you listen to this song, there are two renditions, both sung as a duet. The first rendition has a mellow sound - with a soft tempo and joyful vocals. The second rendition offers folk-style vocals with a matching instrumental.

Listen to the rendition that most resonates with your mood. Ask your spouse to listen with you. Allow your unborn child to hear the music with you. Mary and Joseph are the spiritual parents to everyone in your family. The more you hear this song, the more you can appreciate the depth of God's love and thoughts for a future of hope for you and your family.

Stirring

Duet

Stirring

Duet

A Father's Legacy

Why This Song?

This song is a duet of Mary and Joseph calling and inviting you to believe in their Son Jesus and His love for your family.

You're not just raising children
You're building what will last
Every step you take today
Becomes your future's past

I once laid down my plans to take up something more
I didn't see the harvest yet just seeds upon the floor
But every nail I hammered in
Each prayer I chose to pray
Was shaping what would echo on
Long past my final day

This is a father's legacy
Not gold or fleeting fame
But the truth you plant in quiet hearts
And the love that speaks your name
When the world forgets your footsteps
Heaven still will see
The miracle God builds in time
Through a father's legacy

I watched him hold the weight
Of things he could not say
But in the silence, I could see his faith light up every day
Our Son became a Savior
But first He learned to stand
By watching how a man can love
With work-worn, faithful hands

This is a father's legacy
Not loud or always seen
But the quiet way you listen close
When your family dreams you don't need to be perfect
You just need to believe
That God is writing something great
Through your father's legacy

The world may chase achievement
But Heaven honors grace
The man who walks with mercy
Who leads with patient faith
One day your child will look at you
And see more than just a man
They'll see the road that shaped them
By your steady, open hands

Mary: When you choose to stay and lead them
Joseph: When you love them through the pain
Both: God is carving out a future

Where your sacrifices remain
You don't need to see the ending
Just be faithful where you stand
For every legacy begins
With a willing, open hand

So walk with holy courage let your heart remain sincere
Your prayers will reach
Beyond your life
And echo through the years
One day they'll say your name with joy
And bless the path you gave
Because you led them toward the Light
And taught them how to stay

This is a father's legacy
It's more than just today
It's the quiet love, the sacred fight
To show your child the Way
God is in the moments
That no one else can see
But Heaven sings in honor
Of your father's legacy

A Father's Legacy

Reflection

A father's legacy. This entire book is a resource for you to create a legacy for your family. A legacy of love, not fame, power, status or financial wealth. A legacy of truth, peace and grace that endures for generations.

A legacy, that when you are dying, you look back on your life with peace and joy, knowing that your family was taken care of, protected, guided and led by your caring heart. You are composing the song of your family through the way you live and treat them.

Song Insights

Consider these refrains from the song:

This is a father's legacy, not gold or fleeting fame, but the truth you plant in quiet hearts, and the love that speaks your name. When the world forgets your footsteps, Heaven still will see the miracle God builds in time through a father's legacy. Remember Whom you represent to your unborn child–your Heavenly Father.

This is a father's legacy, it's more than just today, it's the quiet love, the sacred fight to show your child the Way. God is in the moments that no one else can see. But Heaven sings in honor of your father's legacy. In the final analysis, it's not what people think, it's about what God thinks of how you treated the gift of family He has given you.

An Invitation to Listen

As you listen to this song, there are two renditions, both sung as a duet. Both renditions offer stirring vocals and dynamic matching instrumentals.

Listen to the rendition that most resonates with your mood. Ask your spouse to listen with you. Allow your unborn child to hear the music with you. Mary and Joseph are the spiritual parents to everyone in your family. The more you hear this song, the greater you can desire to leave a legacy of love for your family that will last far past your time on earth.

Song of Our Marriage

Gentle

Duet

Why This Song?

This song imagines the love song that Mary and Joseph would sing together to celebrate their marriage.

Giver of beauty
You've entered My life
I thank God every day
That you are My wife
You're filled to the brim
With goodness and grace
Come join me
in love's sweet embrace

Teacher of Wisdom
You've shown me God's face
Your strength is so gentle
And fine as white lace
You listen with heart strings
That sing out a song
It's Your love
That makes me feel strong

Lover of nature
The sun's in your hair
All the meadows of flowers
Could never compare
The treasure you carry
Shines out in your eyes
To make me thank God
You're alive

Teacher of Wisdom
You've shown me God's face
Your strength is so gentle
And fine as white lace
You listen with heart strings
That sing out a song
It's Your love
That makes me feel strong

Prayers so simple
That you whisper now
Move heaven and earth
n my spirit somehow
My joy's overflowing,
My eyes filled with tears,
To have you
And hold you so near

Teacher of Wisdom
You've shown me God's face
Your strength is so gentle
And fine as white lace
You listen with heart strings
That sing out a song
It's Your love
That makes me feel strong

Held and beholden
You make up My dreams
The life we have chosen
Is more than it seems.
We're married forever
With God as our guide
I will always be with you
At your side
I will always be with you, My Bride
I will always be with you, My Bride
Teacher of Wisdom
You've shown me God's face
Our strength is so gentle
And fine as white lace
We listen with heart strings
That sing out a song
It's God's love
That makes our marriage strong

Song of Our Marriage

Reflection

What was the marriage of Mary and Joseph like? How did they honor and treat each other? The little eyes of Jesus were watching them, learning about the human love of husband and wife.

Their Son later taught His disciples about love, how His Father, from the beginning, He made woman and man, to become one flesh and let no other person separate what God has joined. *(Matthew 19:5-6)* What love did Jesus witness in His human parents that reinforced His teaching?

Song Insights

This song models the love and respect that Joseph and Mary had for each other. Their lives were a duet of song, bringing the music of marriage to a rich fullness. Consider these lines from the song:

Teacher of Wisdom, you've shown me God's face, your strength is so gentle and fine as white lace. You listen with heart strings that sing out a song, it's your love that makes me feel strong.

Listening, gentleness, love make for strength.

Held and beholden, you make up my dreams, the life we have chosen is more than it seems. We're married forever with God as our guide, I will always be with you at your side, I will always be with you, my Bride.

The truth is that God marries each of us, and is always with us, just like Mary and Joseph were with each other.

An Invitation to Listen

There is just one rendition, sung as a duet. The song offers gentle and joyful vocals.

Listen to this song with your spouse Allow your unborn child to hear the music with you. Mary and Joseph are the spiritual parents to everyone in your family. The more you hear this song, the greater you will appreciate God's love in your marriage, for you and your spouse.

Our Family is Born Today

Gentle

Duet

Why This Song?

This song imagines a duet by Mary and Joseph sung at the birth of their Son, Jesus. Celebrate their joy with the new family God is giving you.

Joseph
Our little boy is born tonight
In this place so far from home
Yet here the Star of David shines bright
So distant from all we own

Mary
I remember when the angel came
And said I would have a son
An angel gave you His name
Jesus, our babe, our little one

Duet
Our family is born today
Amid the sheep, the straw, the hay
Asleep in our arms now
One day, to Him, all will bow

Mary
The world seems so right and calm
Like we are held in our God's palm
Our little precious boy
Will turn all sin into joy

Joseph
I almost sent you away
Then the angel said, Let her stay
Take Mary your wife into your house
God picked her to be your spouse

Mary
My soul is filled with joy
To hold our little boy
Asleep, after His birth
May He bring peace to all on earth

Duet
Our family is born today
Amid the sheep, the straw, the hay
Asleep in our arms now
One day, to Him, all will bow

Joseph
My love for you is so pure
I'll do my best to keep you secure
I've answered our God's call
To you, my wife, my child, my all

Mary and Joseph
I love you, Joseph, my dear
I feel your heart so near
God's family is born today
He will guide us on the way

Duet
Our family is born today
Amid the sheep, the straw, the hay
Asleep in our arms now
One day, to Him, all will bow

Joseph
Our little boy is full of light
Here the Star of David shines bright

Mary
In manger crude, we pray
Our family is born today.

Our Family is Born Today

Reflection

Imagine what you will feel when your baby is born! That time will offer you a joy you can't describe or explain. A brand new, never before, baby is entering this world. A unique person who is another glimmer of God's glory.

This song models the joy sung by Mary and Joseph when Jesus was born–their Holy Family was alive. And that Holy Family has inspired millions and millions of people since, and touches your family.

Song Insights

Take some time to think about the verses and duet singing in this song. What will you and your wife remember about your family's history?

I almost sent you away, then the angel said, 'Let her stay. Take Mary your wife into your house, God picked her to be your spouse.' God picked you to be your wife's husband, conceive a child, and become a father.

Our family is born today amid the sheep, the straw, the hay. Asleep in our arms now, one day, to Him, all will bow. Mary and Joseph sensed their child's destiny, a destiny of greatness in God's eyes.

My love for you is so pure, I'll do my best to keep you secure, I've answered our God's call, to you, my wife, my child, my all. Joseph sings his promise to Mary of his love, devotion and protection.

An Invitation to Listen

There is just one rendition of this, sung as a duet. The song offers gentle, yet strong vocals - like a lullaby, with a soft tempo and joyful vocals.

Listen to this song with your spouse. Allow your unborn child to hear the music with you. Mary and Joseph are the spiritual parents to everyone in your family. The more you hear this song, the more you will appreciate the great joy of family that Mary and Joseph had when Jesus was born. And expect that joy when your family is born today.

Let Me Sing My Music

Sweet Duet — Tender Duet

Why This Song?

This song is a duet of Mary and Joseph inviting you to sing out the music in your heart for your family, like they had for the Holy Family.

Lyrics

In the quiet of each moment
When I feel joy arise,
With every little heartbeat
I see the world through your eyes.
My love, I'll sing these moments
Let the melody flow
For you and our sweet baby
It's a love we'll always know

So let me sing my music
Let every note be true,
A symphony so joyful
For just me and you
With every dream we're weaving
And every tear we share
I'll sing my love forever
For every moment I care

Through the sleepless nights ahead I'll
hold you close and tight
With whispers of our future,
I'll be your guiding light
Together we'll be dancing
As our little one will grow,
In this song of life and love
We'll let our spirits show

So let me sing my music
Let every note be true,
A symphony so joyful
For just me and you
With every dream we're weaving
And every tear we share
I'll sing my love forever
For every moment I care

As the stars above us twinkle
My heart beats just for you,
With dreams of all tomorrow
And promises so new
I'll serenade our baby
With lullabies so sweet
In the harmony of family
Our lives will be complete

So take my hand, my darling
Let's make this journey bright
With every song we sing
We'll find our love in light.
No fear can hold us back
As we share this sacred sound,
In the music of our hearts
Our happiness is crowned.

So let me sing my music
Let every note be true,
A symphony to cherish
For just me and you
With every dream we're weaving
And every tear we share
I'll sing my love forever
For every moment I care

Let Me Sing My Music

Reflection

Have you ever heard the meme, "Don't die with your music still inside you?" Many people play it too safe in life that they don't let the best of themselves–their love, joy, and presence–get out into the open. Getting the best of yourself into the open blesses you and others.

Think of the love that Joseph and Mary had for each other, that they lived throughout their earthly life, and now together in Heaven.

You are composing a legacy of love for your unborn child, your wife, and yourself. That legacy will impact generations to come, if you don't let it die inside you. Sing your music, now and always.

Song Insights

Imagine what these lines and verses mean to the legacy of love you are composing:

So let me sing my music; let every note be true, A symphony so joyful for just me and you. With every dream we're weaving, and every tear we share, I'll sing my love forever for every moment I care. The music you sing can be a symphony so grand, your heart will feel moved to joyful tears.

So take my hand, my darling, let's make this journey bright, with every song we sing, we'll find our love in light. No fear can hold us back as we share this sacred sound, in the music of our hearts, our happiness is crowned. The music of love has its own reward that touches your life and those around you.

An Invitation to Listen

As you listen to this song, there are two renditions, both sung as a duet. The first rendition has a sweet, romantic, fun sound - with an upbeat tempo and joyful vocals. The second rendition offers tender vocals with a matching instrumental.

Listen to the rendition that most resonates with your mood. Ask your spouse to listen with you. Allow your unborn child to hear the music with you. Mary and Joseph are the spiritual parents to everyone in your family. The more you hear this song, the more music you can witness as you compose a legacy of love for your unborn child and family.

Composing a Legacy of Love

Carry the Day for Your Pregnancy!

"You formed my inmost being; you knit me in my mother's womb. I praise You, so wonderfully You made me; wonderful are your works." Psalm 139:13-14.

Your Pregnancy is About Honoring and Loving New Life
God loves and treasures you, your partner, and your baby! Your pregnancy is a very special time of love. It is the beginning of life for your baby and a precious time for you and your partner to love and bond with your baby and each other. You are becoming a father with a heart of virtue. Your love carries the day for your family.

God is making a brand new human being inside your partner's womb. Her body is creating and sharing life with your baby. God creates your baby's soul. Every day, your baby is growing bigger, stronger, and more beautiful. Every day, your baby is getting ready for the day to enter the world where you and your partner can touch and see.

Made in God's Divine Image
God has made you and your partner in God's Divine Image and God is making your baby in the Divine Image too. Three treasures flow from God's Divine Image: the treasure of being, the treasure of doing, and the treasure of sharing.

God is the source of all life, the treasure of all being. Right now, God is giving existence to your baby with and through you. God is the Creator, the source of all doing, Who does all things. Right now, your partner's body is doing God's work of creating your baby's body. God is the source of all sharing, living together through a community of loving persons–the Father, Jesus the Son, and the Holy Spirit. Right now, your partner is sharing life with your baby through every heartbeat.

God has given you and your partner the gift of life and is working with and through both of you to bring a new life to the world. That life is starting in your partner's womb as an unborn child. When your baby is born, you and your partner will be, do, and share life together with your child as he/she grows and develops.

We'll dive deeper into the three treasures on page 53, but first, read the pages on *Honoring: A Legacy of Treasuring*, starting on page 49.

Honoring: A Legacy of Treasuring

To show honor to God, yourself, and another person is to show deep respect. Honoring is the outward sign of a treasuring heart.

A treasury is a secure place to keep valuable things of great worth. Having a treasury allows you to bring out and invest those valuable things so that they can grow into greater wealth. The treasurer is the person who collects and dispenses the treasure. During your pregnancy, you and your partner are the treasurers who invest love in your baby.

This book offers a treasury of loving words and songs, a collection of valuable things to share with your unborn child and your partner. You don't keep these words to yourself. You invest them in your family. You voice your words with enthusiasm, tenderness, and gentleness so your family can grow into greater human beings. Your love writes a legacy to your partner and unborn child.

What A Legacy of Words and Songs is For

This treasury of words and songs is a resource for you to compose your legacy of love during this pregnancy. It is your "treasuring chest" for ideas, inspiration, and action to express your positive thoughts and feelings as you walk the pregnancy journey with your unborn child and with your partner.

Your thoughts, feelings, words, and actions have a direct impact on partner, which then affects your baby's growth. Your thoughts and feelings influence the words you use when you communicate. When you share positive feelings and words with your partner and baby, spoken or sung, they feel loved, wanted, and treasured. Your partner feels safe. Your baby feels safe. However, if you create an atmosphere of constant negative feelings, you will stress out your partner and harm your baby's ability to trust and grow.

Treasure Your Partner First

Trust is important to receiving and giving love. According to psychologist Erik Erikson[1], trust is the very first stage of human development. Your baby learns to trust or mistrust during infancy–from conception to 18 months after birth. During pregnancy, your partner's body is teaching your baby to trust or mistrust life.

Trusting babies become trusting children and then trusting adults. Mistrusting babies can carry that mistrust throughout their lives and struggle with many problems. That's why you need to treasure your partner first. Please choose to help your partner and your baby feel safe during pregnancy and after birth.

Creating Moments and Memories to Cherish

The latest findings by prenatal psychologists[2] confirm unborn babies are conscious very early in the womb. God creates your baby's soul that is present at conception. Opening up your treasures of being, doing, and sharing feed your baby's soul, much like your partner is feeding your baby's body with her body. God chose you to be the father for this loving task.

Your baby will form memories during his/her time in your partner's womb. From the earliest days of life, those memories collect as cells distributed throughout his/her body, not in the brain. Those cellular memories[3] will last throughout your baby's life. Positive, happy memories of love will help your baby grow and develop with a sense of safety, calm, and connection.

Negative, unhappy memories will hinder your baby's growth and development and lead to anxiety, insecurity, and depression. Conscious intervention and treatment can heal cellular memories can be healed after birth. But why put your partner and your baby in that position, if you don't have to?

You and your partner have the power to create positive memories through the moments you create with your baby. Every small act that you do, sharing thoughts, feelings, and words of love, is a holy moment. Holy moments[4] release oxytocin, the bonding hormone, into your partner's bloodstream, which bathes your baby with positive feelings.

The Heath brothers (Chip and Dan) provide the readers of their book, *The Power of Moments*,[5] with a road map to create defining moments in their lives. Years later, you can revisit defining moments with a smile in your heart. You can enrich your life, connect with others, and make fond memories. Memories that serve your child years after birth.

Composing a Legacy of Love

This section of the book introduces you to the key concepts of living epiphany: treasuring God, yourself, your partner, and your baby. You will learn about the three treasures every human being carries, what love is, your three strands of faith, love, and hope, the LOVE Compass, your treasuring community, and much more. Read this section to learn how to lift up your family during your pregnancy journey.

Treasuring Prayers

Before you can carry your family, you need to allow God's love to carry you away. Prayer is the act of letting God do that through listening and talking. During your pregnancy, you will witness your baby growing within your partner. You will feel a sense of wonder and awe of God's marvelous work. Talk to God in your own words. God is listening, speaking, and communicating with you all the time. Write a sentence or two to God. Read it out loud.

Treasuring Words

We communicate with words. This section of the book gives you the resources to use uplifting, positive, and loving words to honor God, your partner, your baby, and yourself.

Affirm your partner, the mother of your baby. Your pregnancy is a time to grow deeper in love with each other. Your partner needs to know that she is important to you and your growing family.

Talk to your baby often. Find a private place to speak out loud. Use kind words to value and encourage him/her. Use treasuring words to talk to your baby.

Talk to yourself. Affirm how what a loving partner you are and the good father you are becoming. Encourage yourself. You can do this. Appreciate this grace filled time to grow deeper in love.

Treasuring Songs

This part of the book contains 29 simple songs you can sing to honor your baby to grow and be well on the pregnancy journey.

Your baby can hear voices during the last three months of your pregnancy, but feels your partner's emotions throughout your entire pregnancy. When you make your partner happy, your baby is happy too. You and your partner can sing simple songs of God's love to help your baby grow in peace and love. Visit the *Treasuring Songs* section on page 115. Choose one of these songs to sing to your baby. Or compose your own song. See page 159. Then, start singing!

Your Treasuring Action Pages

The *Treasuring Action Pages* are a precious part of your pregnancy journey. This is the space to create a weekly treasuring plan, love your partner as she wants to be loved, and write your thoughts, feelings and messages to God, yourself, your partner, and baby.

As an expecting dad, your place and presence matter. Your partner looks to you for love, care, and support. Pregnancy is a time of drastic change for women. Your partner's body changes. She may be sick at the beginning or throughout the nine months. Her emotions can be more up and down, like a roller coaster.

You need to be present and offer your love more intentionally. During each week of pregnancy, you will put your love into action with a treasuring plan.

Writing your thoughts and feelings is a healthy way to witness the wonder in your pregnancy. You can speak your words out loud to affirm your baby and your partner. Both need to hear the love in your voice. There are two journal pages for each week of your pregnancy journey. Just as your unborn child is growing, watch how your peace, joy, and love for God and life grow deeper and stronger.

The Power of Tiny Habits

Your unborn child begins life as a tiny baby, the union of two cells. Barely visible.

Love starts the same way. Tiny. Too much, too soon, can be overwhelming. This treasury of loving words and songs helps you build a tiny habit[6]–a tiny way of behaving that can grow into a strong bond that lasts a lifetime. Love starts like one of the three strands of your baby's umbilical cord. As small as human hair that grows larger and larger into a rope. See page 59.

When you do something small every day, it becomes a way of living. You can use this treasury to sing one song, say one word, write one sentence in your journal to express your love to God, your partner, your unborn baby, and yourself.

When you do this regularly, that "a little at a time" will grow bigger. You will feel more confident and able to do the larger things you will need to do after your baby is born.

Living Epiphany: Treasuring Begins

"On entering the house, they saw the child with Mary, his mother. They prostrated themselves and did him homage. Then they opened their treasures and offered him gifts of gold, frankincense and myrrh." Matthew 2:11.

The Gospel of Matthew in the Bible tells the story of The Epiphany.[7] Magi from the east come to Israel looking for a newborn king. They find the infant Jesus in Bethlehem and opened their treasures to honor Him. The magi carried their treasures, so the could give gifts. They gave three gifts of gold, frankincense, and myrrh. Valuable gifts kept by kept by Jesus' parents, Joseph and Mary.

This story contains several truths that align with your pregnancy. First, life is a journey and so is pregnancy. You and your partner are journeying through nine months of time to see a newborn baby of great value, and you open up your treasures to give gifts.

God creates every human being God's Divine Image. Every person receives the treasure of being, the treasure of doing, and the treasure of sharing. We carry these gifts throughout our entire life. You and your partner have these treasures and so does your unborn baby. The following pages describe and outline each treasure.

During pregnancy, you will have an epiphany or two. Epiphany means manifestation. Human beings discover what God uncovers. You will discover the wonder of a new human life that God is creating with you and your partner for nine months. Your heart will develop a deeper love for your partner. Both of you will have the honor of sharing a child with your family, a new person of tremendous value that never existed before without you.

Only God knows what your child will become; what things he/she might accomplish, and what he/she will share with the world throughout his/her lifetime. You and your partner will see the mystery unfold and witness the miracle of grace happen during your baby's birth and the days afterward.

You will see the splendor of God's love and joy come to life in a new way for you and your family. You and your partner are a wonderful work of God and so is your baby. Let's explore the three treasures your baby receives and starts to develop during your pregnancy.

The Treasure of Being

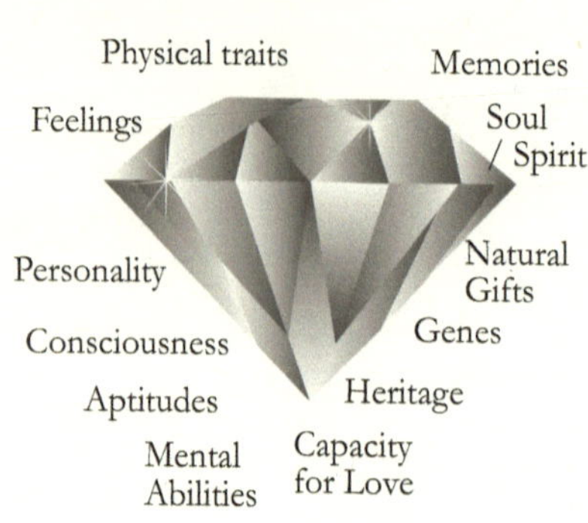

Your baby's treasure of being carries all those gifts that lie at the core of his/her personality and existence.

In your partner's womb, your baby's life, personality, and more begin developing. It will take years for your baby to develop these gifts.

As a dad, you will have the privilege and honor of helping your baby grow this treasure.

Some facets of your baby's treasure of being include:

- Her physical traits like body size and shape; skin, eye, and hair color; his unique fingerprints, vocal cords, and voice patterns; and more.
- Your baby's learning style: visual, auditory, or kinesthetic.
- His personality tendencies, like introvert/extrovert, and more.
- Her aptitudes or natural gifts, like structural or abstract thinking, pitch discrimination, color perception, and more.
- His heritage and genes that spring from previous generations.
- Her soul and consciousness, that God creates and makes her a unique human being.

As parents, you and your partner receive the ability to help your child develop and protect her/his treasure of being for a full and happy life.

The Treasure of Doing

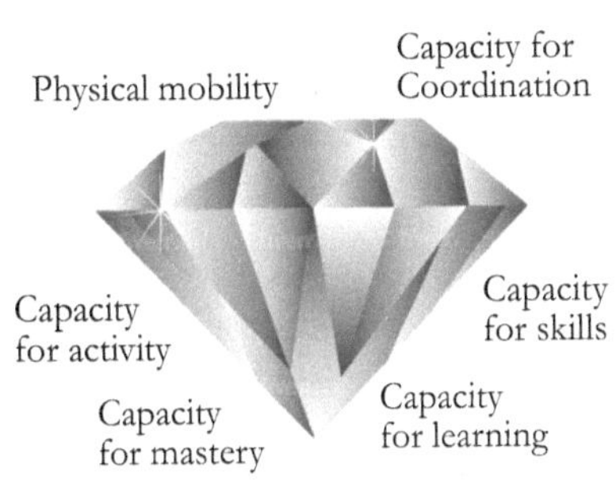

Your baby's treasure of doing carries all those gifts that lie at the core of his/her ability to direct and control the actions of its body and mind.

In your partner's womb, your baby's physical and mental abilities begin. It will take years for your baby to develop these gifts.

As a dad, you will have the privilege and honor of helping your baby grow this treasure.

Some of your baby's treasure of doing include:

- Her physical mobility, flexibility, balance, capacity for strength, and more.
- Your baby's capacity for activity, including focus, concentration, and planning.
- Her capacity for coordination of mind and body.
- His capacity for mastery.
- Her capacity for specific skills and interests in subjects.
- His capacity for learning to do things that come naturally to him.

As a dad, you receive the ability to help your child to develop and protect her/his treasure of doing for a full and happy life.

Your pregnancy is an excellent time to read and learn more about encouraging your child to exercise its treasure of doing.

The Treasure of Sharing

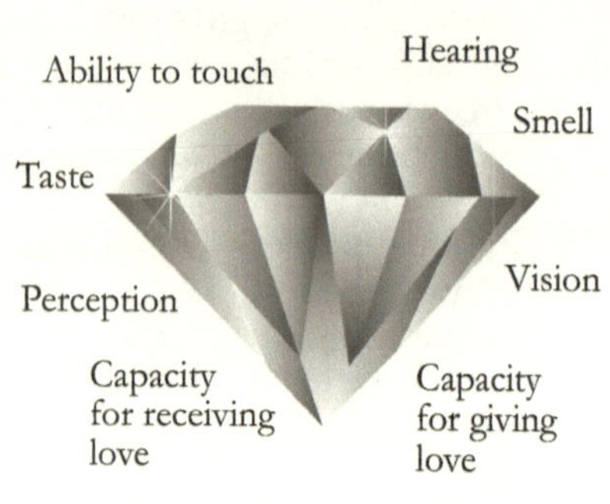

The treasure of sharing is carries the ability to form loving relationships with God, the world, and others. Sharing happens when we are being and doing things *together.*

In your partner's womb, your baby's sharing abilities begin. It will take years for your baby to develop these gifts.

As a dad, you will have the privilege and honor of helping your baby grow this treasure.

Some of your baby's treasure of sharing include:

- Her ability to learn and use her five physical senses, like sight, hearing, touch, taste, and smell. It is through these senses that she gathers information about her environment and people.
- Your baby's capacity to receive love from God, you, and others. Your baby develops its beliefs about safety, security, being wanted, and loved in the womb.
-
- His capacity to give love, based on his feelings of love received during your pregnancy.
- Her very beginning perceptions of what is possible and safe to share.

As parents, you and your partner help your child develop and protect the treasure of sharing. This leads to a full and happy life. Studies show that long-term happiness comes from stable, loving relationships. The first relationships with human beings are with your partner and you.

Attributes of Love

"Love is patient, love is kind. It is not jealous, [love] is not pompous, it is not inflated, it is not rude, it does not seek its own interests, it is not quick-tempered, it does not brood over injury, it does not rejoice over wrongdoing but rejoices with the truth. Love bears all things, believes all things, hopes all things, endures all things. Love never fails." 1 Corinthians 13:4-8.

God's love carries us throughout life. St. Paul's First Letter to the Corinthians spells out these attributes of love. This Scripture passage is often read at weddings, yet it applies to the love you experience during your pregnancy journey.

Love is patient. A normal pregnancy lasts about 40 weeks or nine months. Your baby will grow very at first and then more rapidly just before birth. Good growth takes time. Take things one day at a time. Treasure each moment.

Love is kind. Your baby is fragile, vulnerable, and tiny. Be gentle with your partner and your child. It's okay to be soft-hearted, to speak soothing words.

Love is not: jealous, pompous, inflated, rude, seeking your own interests, quick-tempered, or brooding over injury. Love is not about what you want, think, or feel. Love is serving your partner's and your baby's growth and well-being.

Love bears all things, believes all things, hopes all things, and endures all things. All things. There are no gaps or missing parts. Love doesn't miss a beat. Love is the heartbeat of God in you, your partner and in your baby. God is always working out what is best for all of you, whether the skies are sunny or when life gets stormy.

Love never fails. God's love works miracles. God is love. Even when we humans make mistakes, sin, or miss the mark, God's love restores and makes things right in God's time.

God is calling you, your partner, and your baby to a lifetime–yes, an eternity of love. There is a wonderful life ahead for your family. And there is more–you are loving, lovely, and beloved. Turn the page to learn about who you are becoming.

Loving, Lovely, and Beloved

Your pregnancy is a journey of love. During this journey, you will discover three things about life: yourself, your partner, and your baby. You are loving. You are lovely. You are beloved.

Love is more than just feelings. Love involves a decision to give up some things for the sake of something better. Giving up does not mean quitting. Giving up means going up and growing up–deciding to be loving. God lifts us up to carry us in His love. Then, we carry each other.

You are Loving!
Loving is sacrificing. You may have to give up your own plans, nights out with the guys, personal things that you would rather do. You will have to give up any habits or behaviors that affect your partner's health or emotional well-being. You will need to be patient, kind, and gentle when you feel like yelling or getting angry. Your time will be absorbed by keeping your partner stress-free. At the end of your pregnancy journey, you give again–your time and attention to your newborn baby.

Your Partner is Lovely!
Your partner's body and appearance will change. She will gain weight. Her face may break out with acne. Her body chemistry will change. It's natural. Hang in there. She is still lovely, no matter what she sees in a mirror. In fact, she is more beautiful than she can imagine. Love does that!

You are Beloved!
Your partner's feelings will be like a roller coaster. One minute, she feels exuberant. The next, she might feel anxious or depressed. That is normal. She will have good days and she will have not-so-good days. So will you. You are more than these feelings. No matter how or what you feel, you and she are beloved by God. God the Father loves you, Jesus loves you, and the Holy Spirit loves you. Remind yourself of that regularly.

When fears and doubts visit your partner during your pregnancy, remember: You are loving. She is lovely. All of you are beloved. Love flows from God's love for your family, just like life flows into your baby through three strands. Turn the page to learn more about your three strands.

Three Strands: A Lifeline to God's Love

"A three-ply cord is not easily broken." Ecclesiastes 4:2.

Your unborn baby begins life as a fertilized ovum that travels through your partner's Fallopian tubes into her uterus. It finds a home on the wall of her uterus and a placenta forms. An umbilical cord connects your baby to your partner's placenta.

The typical umbilical cord contains three blood vessels–two arteries and a vein. All the healthy things your baby needs–blood, oxygen, and food–come through the vein from the placenta. All the waste products leave through the arteries to be discharged. Your baby can't survive without your partner's body. Your baby can't live without the three strands, the three blood vessels in the umbilical cord.

The umbilical cord is your baby's lifeline. At first, the blood vessels are as thin as a strand of hair from your head. As your baby grows, the umbilical cord grows bigger and stronger. The arteries and vein grow larger to handle the demands of your baby's growing body. At the time of your baby's birth, the umbilical cord is as thick as a rope. The doctors cut the umbilical cord when your baby is born.

There is Strength in Numbers

A three-ply cord is not easily broken.[8] You have a lifeline–a love line –that connects you and your partner to God's love that is made of three strands. Those three strands are faith, hope, and love. All three strands are God's gift to honor you and to help you stay connected. Faith helps you believe God is alive and with you. Hope helps you expect to receive the good things God is making and doing for you. God's love helps you become the loving, lovely, and beloved family that you are.

Just like your baby's umbilical cord, your love line of faith, hope, and love will grow bigger and stronger throughout life. Your connection to God will become stronger and thicker each day unless you choose to cut the love line. Please honor God by keeping your connection to God, your love line, intact.

God wants you, your partner, and your baby to be happy and

healthy, full of love, life, and light. After birth, your baby will grow to live independently and will have his/her own relationship with God. Your child will have a lifeline of faith, hope, and love that is independent of yours. You and your partner will help your child grow in faith, hope, and love.

There are three persons in every human relationship: yourself, another person, and God. God exists in Three Persons: the Father, Jesus the Son, and the Holy Spirit.

During your pregnancy, you can nourish your partner by speaking her language. You can strengthen your baby's love line to God through your prayers, your words, and your songs. Your baby will learn about God's love through you and your partner.

You have an awesome role as a dad. You are awesome!

Take care of your three strands of faith, hope, and love. Keep them intact. They are your lifeline–and your love line–for a blessed life for you and your family. To remind yourself, read the My 3 Strands for Dads prayer, found below, often.

Love is the greatest of these three strands. Love is the guiding force to your pregnancy journey. The LOVE Compass shows you how to navigate your way to a healthy, happy life.

My 3 Strands for Dads

A child and father, with God's hands,
knit a union of 3 Strands.
Three cords of love, faith and hope
weave a tighter bond than rope.
One greater love, a braid of three,
formed by God, my child and me.
May my 3 Strands be always near;
my child, my gift with God is here.

The LOVE Compass

Every journey has a starting point and a destination. To reach your destination, you need to navigate. Treasuring your unborn child is a journey of your heart. You navigate when you carry and use a LOVE Compass.

A mapping device has four directions: north, south, east, and west. The needle of the geomagnetic compass turns and points to true north.

The LOVE Compass has four movements: listen, observe, value, and express. Instead of a needle always pointing in one direction–true north, your heart turns through four movements.

First, you listen. Then observe. Next, value what you have heard and seen. This person is important to you. Your heart moves you to express your love to that person. During your pregnancy, those persons are God, yourself, your partner, and your baby. As an expecting dad, your priority is to treasure your partner above yourself.

Listen to God's whispers of love, your partner, your baby's movements, your own body, thoughts, and feelings.

Observe what is going on with your partner's body, the calendar, and her stage of pregnancy.

Value the life and tenderness of your unborn child. She/he is fragile, vulnerable, and depends on your love and care.

Express your love by talking to and singing to your child. Smile a lot, take deep breaths, and say prayers to keep your thoughts and emotions positive.

Your heart is at the center of your LOVE Compass. When you use your LOVE Compass, your heart moves through each of the four points. Your heart turns towards the person you are treasuring, not away from that person. When you turn your body toward to face another person, you can hear what is said more clearly. You can observe and see the person as he/she is. You feel more connected. You build a stronger bond in your heart.

When you turn your mind, emotions, and heart toward another person, you feel joy and peace. You carry them with your love.

You open your three treasures–your treasures of being, doing, and sharing–to give the gift of yourself. You have so many gifts that God has given you that you may not even be aware of. The incredible news is that God will give you more gifts to love during your pregnancy. More patience. More kindness. More strength. More ideas and creativity. More compassion. More faith. More hope. More endurance. More belief in life. More love.

The Book of Genesis in the Old Testament of the Bible reveals that human beings are made in the image and likeness of God.[9] We are made in the Divine Image. The writings of John in the New Testament, both his Gospel and the letters of John, say that God is love.

God listens to all of creation, and all of humanity. God observes everything. God values everything that exists because God made it very good.[10] God expresses loving kindness by blessing everything we need to live and grow.

We are made to love and be loved. Love is the great commandment that Jesus taught His disciples: love God with everything you have, with your three treasures, and then love other people like yourself.

Your pregnancy journey starts when God shares life with your partner in her womb. You and she are co-creating a miracle with God–your baby. One day, you will have the absolute joy of looking your baby in the face, seeing his eyes, watching her fuss, feeding, stroking, and touching her/him.

Turn the page to learn the most important use of the LOVE Compass, and how it points the way to treasure God.

Treasuring God: The LOVE Compass

The LOVE Compass guides us to love and treasure God.

We **Listen** to God's Word and God speaking to us in prayer.

We **Observe** God's presence and work in our lives, the world, and history.

We **Value** God as the source of all things, who creates, sustains, and loves everything that exists, seen and unseen.

We **Express** our acceptance and love of God's will and work through our prayers and actions.

We are made in God's Divine Image. When we treasure God in prayer and actions, we express our love to honor God as:

Source of all Being: We Adore God and give God glory, putting God above every power, person, or thing.

Source of all Doing: We Praise God's work and action in redeeming and restoring all creation, including us, to the fullness of our beauty.

Source of all Sharing: We Thank God for what God means to us, what God has done, and what God is doing, and accept the awe of what God will do in the future, together with us.

For All Who God is, we Ask God to help us be, do, and share ourselves and others lovingly with the traits of love on page 57, "*The Attributes of Love.*"

God the Father is like The Almighty Loving Treasure Maker. We are the treasures that God creates, values, and loves. Jesus is like a Master Jeweler, and the Holy Spirit is like a Grand Designer. A diamond sparkles when outside light enters and refracts inside. We sparkle, too–the light of Jesus enters and shines through us. The Holy Spirit guides our actions into God's design of love.

We are like apprentice jewelers; we help polish the jewel of others' lives with our love, so they can shine brighter.

Your Partner and the LOVE Compass

You can use the LOVE Compass to guide you to understand, love, and treasure your partner. Treasuring your partner will help her feel your love so she can relax and focus on being healthy during her pregnancy. You can keep her stress and anxiety to a minimum so that she won't worry about losing your support. That helps your baby be healthy. Healthy mom = healthy baby.

Using the LOVE Compass in your communication with your partner helps you sort out the direction of your words and actions. It is easy to think you know what your partner wants or needs from you. Without going through the process, it's easy to get lost in guessing.

Guessing leads to doubt and forcing your solution to a problem on your partner. Often, it's like trying to fit a square peg into a round hole, to use an idiom. The square peg will never fit, and forcing a fit will damage both the peg and the hole. Using the LOVE Compass with compassion allows you to tune in and be in-the-moment with her.

Tuning In

Tuning out is a danger when your partner needs your attention and care. It is easy to look away when difficult situations arise and not know what is happening with your partner and your pregnancy. Staying focused on her needs is the way you tune in.

Being in the Moment

It is easy to get distracted. Thinking about the past and worrying about the future are distractions. The past is gone and won't be coming back. The future hasn't happened yet and any projections of what might take place aren't certain. Yes, it's important to plan and prepare for the future and include a Plan B; yet we can't control the outcome. The most important moment is the moment happening right now. Some things can wait; some things need attention right now. Be present for the things that need attention now.

The next several pages outline the key concepts of the four movements of the LOVE Compass: Listen, Observe, Value, and Express.

L is for Listen

Remember the game of catch? Speaking is throwing. Listening is like catching. Speaking is the same as sending a message. Listening is receiving that message. Put both actions together, and you begin a conversation.

Loving relationships rely on your communication with each other. Communication is not one way. It involves your loved one sending you a message so you receive and understand her message. Communication that is clear equals a strong relationship.

Listening is receiving words from another person and understanding the message. Listening finds the meaning in those words. Hearing recognizes the sound of a human voice. Listening is the art of understanding what the human voice is saying. On life's journey, you listen to the messages from God, yourself, and other people. You don't just hear a voice.

When you listen, you need a stance to catch the message. Your stance positions your heart to understand what she is saying. A firm stance involves the core elements of openness, focus, willingness, and confirmation. That's it. Just these four elements.

Openness is the ability to receive the words without judging the speaker's worth.

Focus is the ability to stay engaged as long as s/he is talking.

Willingness wants to understand the message.

Confirmation is saying something back to let the speaker know you received the message, and s/he can continue to speak.

A simple conversation may not start that way. A message may be disguised. So how can you take your stance and position your heart to receive a message?

You listen. With your ears, your mind, and your heart. What do you listen to? The loudness and tone of voice tell you if another person is tired, angry, confused, happy, excited, frustrated, or depressed. The energy of voice, how much life or bounce it has, gives you a clue about what another may be feeling.

The choice of words and how those words are said with feeling reinforces the message. What words aren't said? That is a message too.

There are two other areas to listen to your loved one's position in life: your feelings and intuition. Each of these areas helps you understand your loved one's unique journey and your perception of it.

Listening to your feelings is essential to give yourself the chance to clear out pressing emotions that can prevent you from listening closely. One of the biggest barriers to effective listening is missing a message because your feelings speak much louder.

And if all else fails, do the simplest thing. Ask. Ask her how she is feeling. Ask her what she needs right now.

Modern psychologists agree our thoughts have a powerful impact on our emotions. Our self-talk and emotional state flow from our thoughts. Self-talk often takes the form of "I" statements that include the feeling. Each segment of the LOVE Journey during pregnancy can bring out dozens of these personal "I" statements from an expecting mother. Here are some examples.

Fear–"I'm afraid of something going wrong during this pregnancy. What if my baby gets deformed? What if my baby dies? What if my partner gets mad at me, rejects me, or hurts me?"

Anger–"Damn it! Why me? I don't deserve to be sick all the time!" or "I am so mad that this [could be anything] happened!"

Guilt–"If only I would have taken better care of body and my thoughts before I got pregnant, I would never get close to having all these aches and pains. Where did I go wrong?"

Depressed or Sad–"My entire body could pay the price of this pregnancy. Not only will I look ugly, but I'll feel ugly too. I'll never get my figure back again."

Denial–"This entire experience has been like a bad dream. It's not real. I'm tired all the time. I don't have the energy I had before I got pregnant."

Anxious–"I'm really anxious about the doctors discovering something going wrong that I can't fix. What if I can't recover? What will happen to my baby, my family? Will my partner still love me or will he walk out on me?"

Hopeful–"I know I can make it through this. Just one step at a time. I have loved ones who will support me and my body is strong. I will survive this."

Courageous–"I don't care what others say–I'm going to have this baby and this baby will be a blessing to our family!"

Each "I" statement sounds a different tone during the trials of the pregnancy journey. Your partner will have her own thoughts and feelings. Honor her. Tune in to her feelings to appreciate where she is. Listen to what she says and what she doesn't say.

Now that you've heard your partner's story, it's time to see where she's at.

O is for Observe

You need special spectacles when you use the LOVE Compass on life's journey. You need to observe the details, so you don't miss what is hiding.

The English word "observe" comes from the Latin word observāre, which means watch or pay attention to. Like listening, observing is a process. That process discovers what is on the inside. What you observe is on the outside. It is possible to see something and not observe it. Only when you give your full attention to an object is it possible for you to observe it. Like listening, observing is a skill that you can practice, learn, and master. The more you practice, the clearer your observation.

The four core elements are: Notice, Focus, Question, and Realize. When you use these four, you will gain insights you did not see before.

Noticing is being alert to a visual cue that grabs your attention.

Focusing involves your effort to keep your attention on what you see. You watch without interrupting yourself. You don't allow something else to interrupt you.

Questioning is asking yourself about the meaning of what you are watching. Is this important? Why?

Realizing is coming to understand the landscape of what is happening with your partner. As you offer your support during the pregnancy journey, there are several things to observe. Some of these are not apparent.

First, if you have a face-to-face encounter with your partner, observe her body language. What is her body posture? Upright or bowed? Is she close or distant? What is her expression? Frowns, tenseness, tears, smiles? Is she in pain? Her appearance is a signal you cannot ignore.

Second, observe what just happened. Did she have a positive or negative reaction?

Third, observe the time and timing. What is going on with her pregnancy? What did the last visit to the doctor reveal about her health and the health of your baby? Are there anniversaries around the corner? Are there dreaded events ahead?

Add up all the things you observe. Write them down. Ask what this means to you and your partner. Your answer will be in-sight. You will realize what is going on inside. The insights you gain from learning your partner's position come from observing. You become a companion on the pregnancy journey toward your partner's inner beauty and wholeness–which turns into outer health and vibrancy for her and your baby.

Now that you've listened and observed what's going on with your partner, you've learned where she is at. This is the time to value her.

V is for Value

On a LOVE Journey, valuing involves what is on the inside. To value is to discover and appreciate your loved one's inner beauty and worth. Life situations can cause you or others to judge and devalue themselves.

Life makes memories and celebrations; it can also leave scars. A person's self-image can suffer from low value. That is where using valuing is essential. Valuing shows your love for yourself and others. Your value gives her strength for the pregnancy journey.

Like listening and observing, valuing is a skill that you can practice, learn, and master. The more you practice, the more beauty you will see in yourself, your partner, and other people. You will see more beauty that you can express to yourself and others.

The four core elements of valuing are: Recognize, Allow, Reflect, and Engage. R.A.R.E. When you use these four, you will feel more able to behold the priceless nature of yourself and others. You are one of a kind. You, your partner, and your baby are rare. God made only one of you.

Recognizing is coming to know or understand the heart of your loved one and your own heart. You care for her and want to give her support. You want her to journey to well-being and being well.

Allowing allows you to feel how precious other people are. You allow people to be themselves. You accept your partner where she's at. There is an inner glow you receive when you feel appreciated and when you appreciate other people. There is a high value in relationships with yourself and others. Your very presence makes a difference.

Reflecting uses compassion to realize another's inner beauty. No matter what conditions or circumstances may occur. A diamond sparkles because it reflects the light inside itself. Your partner's inner light and beauty make her sparkle in your heart. Your unborn child is a diamond in the making. Your baby is a pearl growing and glowing inside your partner. Your baby is precious too.

Engaging is deciding to share your positive thoughts, words, and actions with yourself and your partner. You begin the process of laying down your life when you engage with others. If you stay aloof and distant, you'll only make a shallow impression.

It takes courage and strength of the heart to make it through the pregnancy journey. You are a faithful companion to your partner. Your words and actions give her the strength to cope and hope. She sees herself as a person of value, because you treat her and your baby like they are valuable.

Now, it's time to *express* the value you see to your partner and your unborn baby.

E is for Express

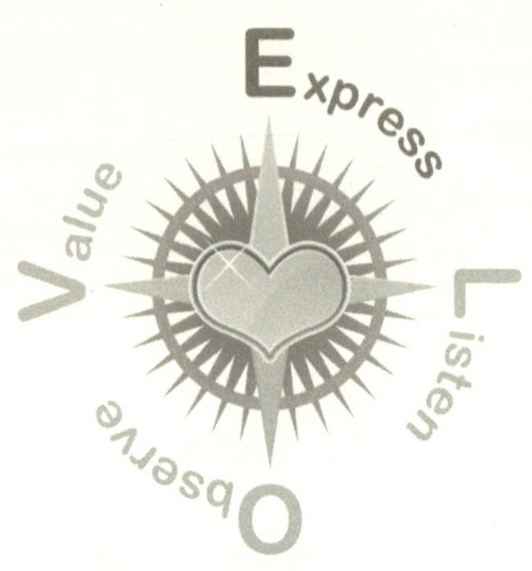

Expressing is sharing heart-to-heart meaning in personal communication. It is the last point of the LOVE Compass. For your partner and your unborn baby, it is the most visible and vital step.

The first three points, Listening, Observing, and Valuing, are as helpful as a daydream without Expressing. You have already listened with attention, observed with insight, and valued with appreciation.

Expressing makes the invisible visible. Your thoughts and feelings become visible to your partner to see, hear, feel, and touch. There are three ways you can express your love, concern, and care: your presence, words, and actions. These are the notes of the score you are composing–the song of love you sing to your life partner and your unborn child–the music of your lives together.

Your Presence

Being present to your life partner and your unborn child combines your physical location, your attention, and your focus. You can be present in your thoughts, even when you are not near your loved ones. You can be far away in your thoughts and attention, even if you are sitting next to them. Choose to engage emotionally as well as physically.

Your Words

The words that you say to yourself and out loud to your partner and unborn child matter. The tone of your voice, the positive or negative emotions, and the words you choose can be life giving or destructive. Choose to be life giving.

Your Actions

What you do to show your care and concern, or apathy, makes memories loving or unloving. Choose to make loving actions.

Composing the Music of Love

Author, pastor and marriage counselor, Dr. Gary Chapman wrote *The Five Love Languages®*. (Learn more about The Five Love Languages on page 325.) Based on these five love languages, there are five corresponding steps[11] to compose the music of love legacy in your relationships with your life partner and your unborn child:

1. Finding the Melody of Connection (Physical touch)
2. Writing Treasuring Lyrics (Words of affirmation)
3. Making the Notation (Gifts)
4. Rehearsing Your Love (Acts of service)
5. Performing in Person (Quality time)

All songs have a *melody*–a series of musical notes that carry the words of the song and are pleasing to hear. Melodies touch the heart and emotions positively. Finding the melody of connection involves finding positive ways to touch your partner in ways she likes and wants.

Lyrics are the words in a song that bring meaning to the melody. Treasuring lyrics are words that admire, encourage, and appreciate another person.

To make music real, so that others can receive the song, the melody and lyrics are written in *notation*. Giving the music away helps others receive and make it their own.

Once you complete the melody, lyrics, and notation, you need to *rehearse* it. Rehearsing involves practicing by acting to serve your partner.

The last stage is *performing in person*–investing your time together. Why do so many people love to go to concerts? They can immerse themselves with the experience of being together for a time with the musical artists.

The next few pages list several ideas for the five different actions involved in composing the music of your pregnancy that you give to your partner. You can add your partner's favorites to the list. You may use all five elements anytime they are pleasing to your partner.

When you reach the *Treasuring Action Plan* pages that begin on page 163, you will write one or more ways to express your love to your partner for each week of pregnancy.

Finding the Melody of Connection

Here is a list of several ideas for ways that you can connect physically with your partner during your pregnancy journey. Check with her to learn what she wants and is appropriate for the time. Add your own ideas to the middle column. Ask your partner to add her favorites to the third column.

Suggested Ideas	Your Ideas	Her Favorites
Give her a hug often.		
Gently massage her arm, neck, back, or legs.		
Hold hands at home and in public.		
Share intimate touching together.		
Place your hands on her baby bump and say, "I love you!"		
Wash and massage her feet.		
Give her a pedicure.		
Stroke her hair.		
Take a shower together.		
Caress her ear lobes.		
Rub lotion on her shoulders.		

Writing Lyrics to Treasure

Here is a list of several ideas for ways you can share your treasuring words to your partner during your pregnancy journey. You can write your own or use others words. See the Treasuring Words section for more details. Add your own ideas to the middle column. Ask your partner to add her favorites to the third column.

Suggested Ideas	Your Ideas	Her Favorites
Greeting cards		
Poems		
Precious Gem poems		
Memes		
Personal love notes		
Word pictures		
Favorite song lyrics		
Admiring messages		
Encouraging messages		
Appreciating messages		
Scripture passages		
Scripture artwork		
Calligraphy		
Inspirational quotes		

Making Notation

Here is a list of several ideas for putting the melody and lyrics on the "paper of your partner's heart" by giving her gifts. The gifts don't have to be expensive; the thought counts when the gift is from you. Remember to smile and give your gift with love. Add your own ideas to the middle column. Ask your partner to add her favorites to the third column.

Suggested Ideas	Your Ideas	Her Favorites
A picture of your growing family.		
A flower.		
A paper heart with her name on it. (Valentine's Day is every day.)		
A favorite sweet or salty snack.		
A scented candle.		
Flavored lip balm.		
Easy-on, easy-off bedroom slippers.		
Her favorite nail polish.		
A bath bomb.		
A little bottle of hand lotion.		
Magazine or book.		
Easy listening music.		

Rehearsing Your Love

Here is a list of several ideas for ways to rehearse the love you are composing by doing things to serve your partner's needs and wants during your pregnancy journey. Add your own ideas to the middle column. Ask your partner to add her favorites to the third column.

Suggested Ideas	Your Ideas	Her Favorites
Vacuum the floors		
Clean the toilets		
Go grocery shopping		
Pay the bills		
Do the laundry		
Take out the trash		
Service the car		
Wash/vacuum her car		
Clean the mirrors		
Do the dishes		
Take dog to the vet		
Drive her to doctor		
Cook dinner		
Dust the furniture		
Change the bed sheets		

Performing in Person

Here is a list of several ideas for ways to perform in person, being present to your partner during your pregnancy journey. This is one-on-one time, where you are connecting with one another (not watching TV or a movie.) Add your own ideas to the middle column. Ask your partner to add her favorites to the third column.

Suggested Ideas	Your Ideas	Her Favorites
Go to her doctor appointments.		
Sit and talk about her, the baby, your family.		
Visit a zoo.		
Take a walk in a park.		
Sit on a park bench together.		
Play cards or a game together.		
Work on a fun or creative project together.		
Carve a pumpkin together.		
Light a candle and pray for yourself, family, and friends together.		
Sit together and talk to your baby.		
Do the "Resting Prayer" together.		

Your Family's Treasuring Community

The good news is that you aren't alone in supporting your partner and your baby on the pregnancy journey. You are in the company of a treasuring community.

There are people who carry you by the love in their hearts. You know some of them. Your parents and grandparents. Your family of origin. Her parents and grandparents. Her family of origin. Your friends and people who know you. Her doctor and medical team. People you don't know who want your pregnancy to go well. There are saints, angels, guardian angels, and people that you haven't met who pray for you and your unborn baby. There are many good men who have gone on the pregnancy journey with their partners. Catholic men can make friends and join the Knights of Columbus. They can mentor you during your journey. Seek them out.

When you need prayer help, turn to the parents of Jesus. Your spiritual mom, Mary, the Mother of Jesus. Her prayers and presence are always with you. All you have to do is to ask Mary for help, wisdom, and strength. She will hear prayers and help you. Mary understands what your partner is going through. She went through pregnancy and childbirth with her Son, Jesus. She loves you and your family.

Ask St. Joseph to pray for you. He is the human father of Jesus and your spiritual father. St. Joseph accompanied Mary during her pregnancy and is the patron saint of families. Read more about St. Joseph in the *Treasuring Prayers* section on page 83. Ask God, your Heavenly Father, Jesus, and the Holy Spirit for whatever help you need. Seek the prayers of the saints, like those mentioned on page 329. You can ask for the love and prayers of your family members who have died and live now in heaven with God. They are the "saints in your corner"–members of your prayer circle who ask God's protection, guidance, wisdom, and love for you.

The Impact of Loving Support

"And the Word became flesh and made his dwelling among us." John 1:14.

Your words, either sung with music or spoken, carry the power to be life-giving. Words express love, care, concern, and support. The emotions you have when you speak or sing your words are important. You want to cultivate and express positive emotions: peace, joy, hope, and love.

Designed for Love

God designs all human beings for love. Love is food for the spirit, just like bread is food for the body. Your unborn child needs your love and acceptance. Prenatal psychologists discovered unborn children thrive when they feel the love of their mothers. Happy mom, happy baby. Loving mom, loved child.

Unborn babies suffer when they lack a father's and mother's love and acceptance, both before and after birth. Stressed out mom, kicking baby, depressed baby. Unhappy mom, unhappy baby. Unloved mom, unloved baby.

An Expecting Dad Causes Stress or Protects Against Stress

One of the biggest causes of stress to expecting moms is the absence, emotional distance, and lack of support from the fathers of their babies.[12] That stress gets worse when their partners pour out anger, impatience, and negative emotions upon them. Your expecting partner is not a punching bag for you. If you have an issue with anger, learn how to handle it constructively so you don't harm anyone, emotionally or physically. An excellent resource is Dr. Gary Chapman's' book, *Anger: Taming a Powerful Emotion.*

What you think, feel, and say to yourself, your partner, and your baby affects your health[12]. High stress, along with constant negative emotions, releases harmful hormones in your partner's body. Your baby can withstand fleeting negative emotions. Constant stress harms all of you.

How do you solve this? Soften the strength and length of negative emotions. Replace them with peaceful, gentle, and loving feelings. Get help if you struggle with constant fear, anxiety, guilt, shame, or self-doubt from past or current relationships. The *Research & Resources* section that begins on page 323 lists several sources of help.

Visualizing Your Baby

Visualizing good things to come, being thankful, and praying are three of the strongest ways to grow positive emotions.

There is nothing so sweet in life as holding a newborn baby. It is a tender, loving moment between a dad and a newborn baby–to touch and hold your newborn baby.

Your partner is holding that baby right now, growing inside her body. In her heart, your partner is using her imagination to get ready for the day when she will touch your baby's skin, see the smile in her/his eyes, watch him/her wriggle its toes, touch her cheek with tiny fingers, and fall sleep on your shoulder.

Right now, the only images of your baby that you can touch are the ultrasound pictures or live ultrasound scans in the doctor's office. Yet, in your imagination, you can visualize those same moments–when you will hold your newborn baby, stroke his/her face, run your fingers through her/his hair, let him/her fall asleep on your shoulder.

You and your partner will have many precious moments where love will fill your heart; tears of joy will streak your cheeks, and love will move you to do things you never thought you could do.

You will know how loving, lovely, and beloved your partner is and how wonderful your family is. More and more each day, you will grow into a loving father who takes care of himself and his family. These will be moments to cherish, moments that money could never buy. Moments that all the power and fame in the world could never replace.

God's Word and Song Became a Baby

The most loving Word ever spoken, the most beautiful song ever sung are those given by God. Jesus is the Word of God–God's love spoken and sung to people for thousands of years. A Word that doesn't fade or die. A Song that never stops nor goes silent. Jesus' mother, Mary, conceived and carried Jesus to birth. Mary is not God, yet she received God's love and grace to express perfect human love for Joseph, her spouse, and Jesus, her unborn child. Mary's love, presence, and prayers are with you and your unborn child during your pregnancy. The next section, *Treasuring Prayers*, will include several resources to help you pray.

There are but three things that last–faith, hope, and love–and the greatest of these is love.

Treasuring Starts in Pregnancy But Doesn't End There
Sharing treasuring messages is a lifelong journey of love that includes God, yourself, and another person. You need to carry out your intentions.

The *Treasuring Action Pages* section of this book will give you the space to create a weekly treasuring action plan during pregnancy. You can choose how you want to love your partner and how to communicate with your unborn child. You can write out messages of admiration, encouragement, and appreciation to God, your partner, your baby, and yourself.

Treasuring doesn't end when your child is born. As a dad, you will be an inspiring presence to your child throughout life. Treasuring is a process you can use to honor a partner, children, parents, siblings, family members, friends–anyone you value–throughout their entire lives.

The most powerful way to treasure and honor others is to bless them. That's what God did in the story of creation. God blessed all creation, including humanity. God gave the power to grow and multiply. Jesus taught His disciples to bless all people, even those who are unloving toward you and others. Read and reflect on the lyrics to the legacy song *Blessing Prayer* on page 340. Bless the ones you love in life.

Remember, God admires, encourages, and appreciates every human being. That includes you, your partner, and your unborn child. It's your turn to do the same. When we admire, encourage, and appreciate ourselves and our loved ones, we help bring heaven to earth. We become God's forever family. Reflect on the lyrics to the inspired legacy song, *Forever a Family*, on page 341.

Treasuring Prayers

Prayer: Letting God Carry You Away

Prayer is the act of speaking and listening to God, Who is eager to carry you away with His love. Prayer is communicating with God, Who is wiser, stronger, more loving, all-knowing, and infinitely good, far above any human being could ever be. God's very first commandment is to honor God above everything else.

God created you, continues to give you life, and loves you personally far beyond what you could ever imagine or visualize. God has that infinite love for all people, including your unborn child. God wants to you to belong to God's forever family–all the moments here on earth and in heaven forever after we die.

There are four ways of praying to God where we do the speaking: adoration, praise, thanksgiving, and petition. God speaks to us all the time; our task is to listen and do what God tells us to do.

God is our Divine parent, Who knows everything about us and gives us what we need to grow. God is so wise that God knows what we need before we even ask. So we can keep it short when we talk to God.

If we need something, we can ask for it. We don't need a lot of words. Or we can talk on and on. It doesn't matter. God listens to our hearts, observes our lives and situations, values us as beloved children, and expresses love by answering what we ask for. In fact, Jesus told his disciples that His God and Father knows what we need before we even ask for it.[13]

You can tell God whatever you want, how good or lousy you feel, how right or unfair life seems to be. You can use a formal prayer, like the Our Father, Hail Mary, Hail Joseph, or the rosary. Or, you can talk spontaneously. You can speak to God out loud or quietly in your mind, and God listens. God cares. God transforms.

When you set aside time to pray to God, you are taking your heart into God's presence. Be quiet and listen to what God is saying to you. God answers your requests, the things you ask for, sometimes right away, sometimes later. Our response is to trust, persist, wait, and listen to the answers that come. God's answers are in time and on time–in God's time, not ours.

Carrying Love Through a Righteous Life

How do you allow God to carry you away with His love, and then carry others with the love God gives you? The three songs on pages 20-25 point out three important ways to practice a righteous life as an expecting dad. A righteous life is living in communion with the three Persons of God: the Father, the Son, and the Holy Spirit. The three ways of living in communion are: Obey the Father, Believe in Jesus, Listen to the Holy Spirit.

Obey the Father

God the Father is the Source of all love and life, Who directs all creation according to His Will and Plan for good. God's wisdom is beyond any human thought or reasoning. The Father created all human beings with free will. We can choose to follow the Father's wisdom or not. When we choose to obey the Father's laws, guidance, commandments, we invite a life of joy and happiness for ourselves and others. When we choose a selfish way, we make life miserable. Choose to Obey the Father. Listen to the song, *Obey the Father*, on page 20 when you need encouragement to do God's will. Say the 'Our Father,' the prayer Jesus taught us to pray, every day:

Our Father, in Heaven, holy is Your Name. Your Kingdom come, Your will be done on earth as it is in Heaven. Give us this day our daily bread. Forgive us our trespasses as we forgive those who trespass against us. Lead us not into temptation, but deliver us from evil. Amen.

Believe in Jesus

The Father sent His Son Jesus, to redeem us from our selfish ways and show us His Father's face. Jesus always obeyed the Father. Jesus died on the Cross to destroy sin and His Father raised Jesus from the dead to new life. When we believe in Jesus, and follow Him, we participate in that new life for ourselves and other people. Choose to Believe in Jesus. Listen to the song, *Believe in Jesus*, on page 22 when you need a boost of faith.

Listen to the Holy Spirit

Jesus promised those who believe in Him, that He would send the Holy Spirit to them as a guide, comforter, and advocate. The Holy Spirit would give spiritual power and life to those who believe in Jesus and follow Him. The Holy Spirit gives spiritual gifts and reminds us of Jesus' words. At the Catholic Mass, the priest asks the Father to send the Holy Spirit to consecrate the bread and wine to become the Body and Blood of Jesus. Choose to listen to the Holy Spirit. Listen to the song, *Listen to the Holy Spirit*, on page 24 when you need inspiration.

Simple Prayers During Pregnancy

Here are several short prayers to get you thinking about talking to God. The idea here is to share situations and words to say. You can make up your own prayers just by speaking what's on your mind and asking God for what you need.

When You Feel Blessed, Happy, or Joyful
Dear God (Father, Jesus, Holy Spirit), thank you for blessing me with ________________. I love you!

When You Feel Stressed, Down, Sad, or Have Trouble
Dear God, I feel so ____________ right now. Please help me with your peace and make things work out right. Thank you. Amen.

When You Need Help with Something
Dear God, my problem is ________________. Please help me with this. Thank you. Amen.

When You Feel Afraid or Anxious
Dear God, I'm feel scared about ___________. Please give me what I need right now. Thank you. Amen.

For Your Partner
Dear God, please give ___________ Your peace, health, and love in every part of her body, mind, spirit and emotions. Keep her safe and bless our pregnancy. Help her become a wonderful mother. Thank you. Amen.

For Your Baby
Dear God, please help our unborn child be healthy and grow in peace and love during this time of pregnancy. Protect our baby and guide us as loving parents. Thank you. Amen.

A Prayer to the Holy Spirit

Come Holy Spirit, fill my heart with the fruits you give
And breathe your grace today in the way I live.
Give me love, joy and peace Make me patient, and kind.
Make me mild and good in every thought of my mind.
Grant me self control to do what's right.
Lead me today with your Holy light. Amen.

Resting Prayer

Your pregnancy journey offers time to rest. As your baby grows larger, your partner will feel more tired. That is normal.

You and your partner can turn your resting time into a resting prayer, where you just sit or lie down in God's presence. You can speak to God in that posture, or just close your eyes and listen. Your partner and your baby are resting with you. This is a precious time to treasure your baby's soul. When your partner practices resting prayer, join her. Invite her to take a break and pray with you.

Here are several suggestions to practice resting prayer.

1. Set aside five to twenty minutes for your resting.
2. Use a timer so you won't fret about when to get up.
3. Find a quiet space where you can sit or lie down with your partner undisturbed. If you are sitting, put both feet on the floor. If you are lying down, stretch out.
4. Let your body relax.
5. Put your hands on your partner's "bump" to invite your baby to rest in God with you.
6. Breathe slowly in and out.
7. Imagine that God is breathing in and out with you. Visualize God's love and peace, covering you like a blanket.
8. Let your thoughts come and go, like watching them float down a river like leaves. Repeat a word, like peace or love.
9. Open your heart to listen to God's words of love speak to you in silence.
10. When the alarm from your timer goes off, open your eyes. Move your arms, legs, and body slowly before you rise.

The more you practice resting prayer, the more your partner, baby, and you will feel refreshed and at peace.

St. Joseph: Father to Expecting Dads

What Makes Up A Father's Heart?
You began reading this book by listening to songs that St. Joseph and Mary would sing of their love for you. Composing a legacy of love during pregnancy and childbirth is more than a journey for your partner and unborn child. This time is a journey to fatherhood for you. Whether this pregnancy is your first time or the twelfth one, you can always grow deeper in love. Love is a journey of the heart. St. Joseph was a just man with a father's heart. God trusted Joseph to carry His Son Jesus. Love belongs to a treasury of nine spiritual jewels that enrich everyday living. A treasury that you carry with you in your heart.

Joseph Loved and Honored His Wife Mary
Joseph faced a dilemma. When he was betrothed to Mary, he learned Mary was pregnant, not by him. At the time, Jewish law was to stone women who committed adultery. Joseph was about to dismiss her quietly, to separate himself, so that she would not be harmed. Then, in a dream, an angel of the Lord appeared to him. The angel announced the reason for Mary's pregnancy: the Holy Spirit had conceived a Son in her. Mary's Son would save people from their sins. Joseph was to take Mary as his wife. Joseph was to name the unborn child Jesus when he was born.

Joseph awoke, took his wife Mary into his home, and walked with her through pregnancy and birth. In fact, Joseph traveled from Nazareth to Bethlehem to fulfill a Roman census, just before Jesus was born. Joseph found a place for Jesus' birth and was present when that happened. Joseph carried his wife and newborn son to safety in Egypt to escape Herod's plan to kill all infant boys. After Herod died, and the angel appeared to Joseph again in a dream, instructing him to return home. Joseph obeyed again and traveled to Nazareth, where he and Mary raised Jesus.[14] Listen to and reflect on the lyrics to the legacy song, *Song of Our Marriage*, page 40. Joseph lived this song with his wife, Mary.

Joseph, Earthly Father of Jesus
Joseph built a legacy of love for his family, using physical tools for his livelihood and spiritual tools for his life. He worked as a carpenter. He was a faith-filled Jew who prayed, read the Torah, and kept God's commandments. He supported his wife and son. Even though Jesus' Father was God, Joseph's love was an

ambassador for God during their earthly lives, full of the fruits of the Holy Spirit. Joseph provided, protected, guided, served, and was present to his family. God's grace calls you to do the same.

Love Stands Out in a Box of Spiritual Tools
Love is the most useful tool to use when raising a family. Jesus was conceived by the Holy Spirit. Jesus was the foster son of Joseph; Joseph taught and raised Jesus. Jesus grew up to gather people, teach them about love, and give the Holy Spirit so that they would love and treasure God, themselves, and others.

In Chapter 5 of his Letter to the Galatians[15], St. Paul lists nine fruits of the Holy Spirit: love, joy, peace, patience, kindness, generosity, faithfulness, gentleness, and self control. The fruits of the Holy Spirit are the spiritual tools that build love in your heart. Their opposites are vices. Practicing and using spiritual tools lead to a fulfilling life for yourself and others. Practicing and living vices lead to behavior that will trap you and others in a grip of destruction.

The heart of a good father is a treasury of the fruits of the Holy Spirit. These fruits are the tools that shape the treasures of being, doing, and sharing. You open your heart to find the spiritual tools and use them to build up your partner and unborn child. During your pregnancy journey, you will have plenty of opportunities to practice and use these spiritual tools. Please choose to do so. The next pages contain several prayers to ask St. Joseph's help.

Prayers to St. Joseph
St. Joseph lived a life of righteousness on earth. Now, he lives with his family in heaven. You can pray to St. Joseph for fatherly help, to for ask his intercession during your pregnancy and life situations. Here are several "formal" prayers you can say. You can talk to Joseph in your own words too, just like you can talk to Mary, the Mother of Jesus. Both of them seek good on your behalf. Play the songs, *We Love You Our Son* and *Always in Your Heart* for inspiration.

Hail Joseph Prayer
This prayer mirrors the Hail Mary prayer to recognize St. Joseph's presence and prayer for you. Say this easy-to-remember prayer often.

Hail Joseph, called by grace.
The LORD dreams with you.
Blessed are you among fathers,
And blessed is the child you raised, Jesus.
Holy Joseph, protector of homes,
Pray for our families now
And when we take our last breath. Amen.

Praying to St. Joseph for Righteous Living

Life's uncertainties, situations, and circumstances can challenge the heart of any expecting dad. It is easy to slip into a vice and get trapped there. A physical vise is a tool a carpenter uses to hold something temporarily so it can be worked on. A spiritual vice works on you to squeeze the love out of your heart. The problem is that vice carries your family along with you. Spiritual vices crush a man's soul, along with his loved ones. During his time on earth, St. Joseph used physical vises for his work and avoided spiritual vices to be free to love and serve his family.

God's grace is available to help you escape the trap of vices and sin. For Catholic men, receiving the Sacraments of Penance and Holy Communion bring forgiveness and freedom. Praying to St. Joseph can help you stay free so you and your family live fully.

Here is a treasury of prayers to St. Joseph asking for his help to practice using the fruits of the Holy Spirit and to get free of vices (no matter how large or small.) Grow a father's heart of grace during your pregnancy and childbirth. Think of the situation that is troubling you the most, then find the prayer that matches your situation. Feel free to change the words that fit your situation, or talk to St. Joseph in your own words.

Love (instead of unforgiveness, resentment, or jealousy)

St. Joseph, I feel jealous (resentful, unforgiving) about __________. You experienced many times when people did unloving things to you and your family. Yet you let those things go and continued to show your love to Mary and Jesus. Please help me love those who are unloving, who appear unlovely, or come across as being unlovable. Pray that I may become a father after God's heart. Thank you for hearing my prayer. Amen.

Joy (instead of discouragement, despair)

St. Joseph, I feel discouraged (sad, depressed) about ______________. You were alone with Mary and the infant Jesus in a strange place without friends. Yet the magi appeared, bearing treasures and gifts from God's providence. Please help me experience joy and hope to see God at work in my circumstances. Pray that I may become a father after God's heart. Thank you for hearing my prayer. Amen.

Peace (instead of worry, anxiety, fear, dread)

St. Joseph, I feel anxious and worried about _____________. You faced an anxious moment when you learned that Mary was pregnant and you didn't know how. Yet an angel appeared to you and explained what was happening. Please help me find peace with this troubling situation. Pray that I may become a father after God's heart. Thank you for hearing my prayer. Amen.

Patience (instead of anger, frustration)
St. Joseph, I feel upset and irritated about ___________. You faced a trial when you had to flee to Egypt because of Herod. yet you continued to protect and support your family. Please help me be patient with this situation. Pray that I may become a father after God's heart. Thank you for hearing my prayer. Amen.

Kindness (instead of rejection, meanness)
St. Joseph, I feel like taking things out on ___________. You faced the temptation to be mean or unkind to the innkeepers who had no room for you when Mary was about to give birth to Jesus in Bethlehem. Yet you kept your cool to find a stable that served as a birthplace. Please help me be kind with this situation. Pray that I may become a father after God's heart. Thank you for hearing my prayer. Amen.

Generosity (instead of selfishness, stinginess)
St. Joseph, I am being selfish with my time, money, and attention toward ___________. You faced those same temptations when you had to give up the comfort of home to travel to Bethlehem to fulfill the census when Mary was expecting. Please help me be generous with my partner, family, and others in this situation. Pray that I may become a father after God's heart. Thank you for hearing my prayer. Amen.

Faithfulness (instead of betrayal, storming out, or leaving)
St. Joseph, I feel distracted and tempted to betray ___________ in my thoughts, words, and actions. You faced those same temptations when you learned Mary had an unexpected pregnancy. You could have sent her away, yet you remained faithful to her and to God's command through the angel. Please help me be faithful to God and others in this situation. Pray that I may become a father after God's heart. Thank you for hearing my prayer. Amen.

Gentleness (instead of criticism, sarcasm, harshness)
St. Joseph, I feel harsh toward __________ in my thoughts, words, and actions. You faced those same temptations whenever you were laughed at, made fun of, or rejected and chose to respond with gentleness. Please help me be gentle with those in this situation. Pray that I may become a father after God's heart. Thank you for hearing my prayer. Amen.

Self control (instead of indulgence, laziness)
St. Joseph, I'm about to lose it by doing ______________. You faced the same temptations to avoid your responsibilities toward God to take care of Mary, Jesus, and yourself when God had other plans for your life. Please help me gain self-control and submit to God's guidance and plan for my life, especially now during this pregnancy. Pray that I may become a father after God's heart. Thank you for hearing my prayer. Amen.

Humility: The Tool Belt Holding Your Spiritual Tools

A treasuring life is the crowning glory of an expecting father. Humility is the 'leather belt' that holds the spiritual fruits of the Holy Spirit so that you can carry and draw them out to use.

What is Humility?

Humility is often misunderstood in today's world. On one hand, being humble is equated with feeling inferior to others: being a doormat, letting others walk all over you. On the other hand, humility is tossed aside by feeling superior to others and looking down on them. Humility is neither. Being humble is a 'heart-set' that recognizes all people have the same worth and value, made in God's Divine Image and treasured by God as precious people. Humility accepts everything in life as God's gift to help us grow.

Vices Against Humility

The three vices that work against humility are arrogance, vanity, and pride. These three vices toss God from the center of our lives and put ourselves there instead. Pride was the original sin of humankind told in the Book of Genesis. Adam and Eve were tempted to become like gods by taking what wasn't theirs and disobeying God. Only God is God. Human beings are not God even if they believe, talk or behave that way. The irony is that God shares Divinity freely–and humans only have to receive it.

What You Wear, Wears Off On Others

Have you ever met someone, and after some time listening or observing, you thought, "This person is full of him/herself." Everything that person said or did was about her/himself. That type of encounter can wear on you. It pushes you away from that person.

Yet, how do you feel when you meet someone who asks about you, listens to you, admires, encourages, or appreciates you? An encounter with that person may attract you, so that you want to spend more time with him/her.

So it will be for you. If you crown yourself and demand others to worship you, the vices of pride, arrogance, and vanity will be your reward. If you let humility rule over your actions, the honor you receive will result in a heart that treasures others.

St. Joseph and Humility

St. Joseph was a man who wore his tool belt of humility as husband of Mary and earthly father to Jesus. He loved and protected his family. He lived faithfully to obey God. The Scriptures don't record any spoken word by Joseph, only the key actions he took to treasure God and protect his family. He was a just man, who loved goodness, and walked humbly with his God.[16] St. Joseph lived as a man for others. He used the spiritual tools to build his family as a blessing for countless people to experience God's gift of love. So you can live for your partner, your unborn child, and other people.

Prayer for Humility

Say this prayer to ask St. Joseph for help to find and wear a tool belt of humility. (You may also go to a deeper level of devotion by consecrating your words and actions to St. Joseph.[17])

> St. Joseph,
>
> You lived a life of service and love for your family. You acted justly, loved faithfulness, and walked humbly with your God. Please pray that I may learn and imitate your humility, so that I may love my partner, my unborn child, and my family during pregnancy, childbirth, and the time afterwards. Thank you for hearing my prayer. Amen.

Prayers to St. Joseph for Work

Working at a job or profession is one of a dad's ways to support and protect his family. St. Joseph worked as a tradesman–a carpenter. He was a displaced worker and had to flee to Egypt with his family when Herod ordered the murder of infant boys. He found and kept work to earn a living wage. He relocated to Nazareth when he, Mary, and Jesus returned to Israel. He put sweat into his work to put bread on the table. You can ask St. Joseph to pray for your work as you provide for your family. Use these prayers or pray in your own words to St. Joseph.

For Daily Labor
St. Joseph, please help me do the tasks at my job with skill, mastery, and diligence. Bless my work today, the people we serve, and the organization I work for. Thank you for hearing my prayer. Amen.

For Stress in the Workplace
St. Joseph, please help me deal with the changes in my workplace and the organization. Let me focus on the work of today, and trust that God will provide for tomorrow. Thank you for hearing my prayer. Amen.

For Seeking Employment
St. Joseph, please help me find a job or position that fits my skills and experience, allows me to serve others, and provides for my family. Thank you for hearing my prayer. Amen.

For Relocation, Downsizing, New Employment
St. Joseph, please guide me to a new place of work or a new position that will help me serve my family. Thank you for hearing my prayer. Amen.

There are many prayers and information about St. Joseph in other books. Page 336 in the *Research and Resources* section lists several sources.

Just like St. Joseph prays for you during your pregnancy, Mary's presence and prayers are with you and your partner on your pregnancy journey. Turn to page 95 to read about Mary's prayers for you during this precious time.

Praying with Mary

Mary, the Mother of Jesus, the Mother of God, is your mother, too. Mary knows how to pray with you and asks God for blessings, protection, and health for you and your family.

Mary Treasured God When She Was Pregnant with Jesus

When Mary was pregnant with her Son, Jesus, she visited her cousin Elizabeth. Elizabeth greeted Mary and called her blessed among women. Mary responded with a prayer of song praising God, now called The Magnificat.[18] You can pray this Scripture passage with Mary to treasure God any time or anywhere

> And Mary said:
> "My soul proclaims the greatness of the Lord;
> my spirit rejoices in God my savior.
> For he has looked upon his handmaid's lowliness;
> behold, from now on will all ages call me blessed.
> The Mighty One has done great things for me,
> and holy is his name.
> His mercy is from age to age
> to those who fear him.
> He has shown might with his arm,
> dispersed the arrogant of mind and heart.b
> He has thrown down the rulers from their thrones
> but lifted up the lowly.
> The hungry he has filled with good things;
> the rich he has sent away empty.
> He has helped Israel his servant,
> remembering his mercy,
> according to his promise to our fathers,
> to Abraham and to his descendants forever."

God is looking upon you during your pregnancy to bless and do great things for you, your partner, and your unborn child. Mary's prayers are always with you. Pray the *Hail Mary* every day:

Hail Mary, full of grace, the Lord is with you. Blessed are you among women and blessed is the fruit of your womb, Jesus. Holy Mary, Mother of God, pray for us sinners, now and at the hour of death. Amen

After Mary's earthly life was over, she went to Heaven to be with God and look after her human family. She has appeared many times during human history to remind people of her presence and prayers.

Mary Appeared as Our Lady of Guadalupe

In December 1531, Mary appeared to Juan Diego at Tepeyac Hill near Mexico City. She came as a young, native Indian, pregnant woman. Mary asked Juan to build a chapel in her honor at that spot. She gave the local bishop a sign, her image on Juan's tilma (or cloak). The tilma still exists and is on display at the Shrine in Mexico City today.

Mary's words of love to Juan Diego echo through the centuries to you and your family for your pregnancy at this moment.

In 1931, for the 400th anniversary of Mary's appearance, Luis Maria Martinez, Bishop of Mexico City, wrote a series of meditations in the book, *Am I Not Your Mother: Reflections on Our Lady of Guadalupe.*[19] He composed a nine-day novena, based on the words Mary spoke to Juan Diego.

The words of the Bishop and Mary address every human person, including our unborn children:

"My child, whom I love as a little and delicate one"–Mary, who knows our strengths and limitations, loves us. How little and delicate are unborn children.

When Juan Diego was concerned about the health of his uncle, he tried to avoid encountering Mary by taking a detour around the spot where they met. She appeared to him anyway and said,

"Listen and understand, my littlest son, let nothing frighten and afflict you or trouble your heart … Am I not here, I, who am your mother? Are you not under my shadow? Am I not your health? Are you not by chance held in my mantle?" Mary's love is gentle. She is always here, with you, your partner, and your child in pregnancy and throughout life as your spiritual mother.

This title of Mary is Our Lady of Guadalupe. She is the patroness of unborn children. For a treasuring song about Our Lady of Guadalupe, read *Las Rosas de Mar*ia on page 342 in the *Appendix: Legacy Songs* section.

Mary is the First Member of Your Prayer Circle

When you ask Mary to pray for you, you can count on her prayers being answered. Talk to Mary as your own loving mom. She wants the best for you. Use simple requests, like:

> "Mother Mary, please help me with this problem."
>
> "Mother Mary, please ask Jesus to send His peace to me and my baby."
>
> "Mother Mary, I need God's help. Please ask God for me!"

On a more formal basis, you can pray the Hail Mary and the Rosary asking Mary to pray for you.

Here is a story that illustrates the power of Mary's prayers.[20]

Once, there was a King who demanded tribute from his subjects. A very poor farmer came to pay his debt. His only possession was a half-rotten apple. The Queen took the farmer's apple, cut out the bad part, sliced up the good part, and arranged the apple slices on a silver tray with rose petals. She went with the farmer and presented his gift to the King, who was delighted with it. The King forgave the farmer's debt and restored the farmer's land.

Mary's prayers work like that by presenting your needs to her Son Jesus–on a silver platter.

One of the most helpful ways to ask Mary's prayers is to pray the Rosary. Read the next few pages for two Scriptural rosaries. These rosaries are based on Gospel stories, from St. Joseph's life during pregnancy and birth

Rosary Reflections for Pregnancy and Birth

Praying the Rosary is an excellent way to ask for Mary's help and prayers during your pregnancy. Mary was pregnant with Jesus for nine months. Then, she gave birth to Him. Mary's prayers are always with you.The next three pages contain Scriptural rosaries for pregnancy and birth, based on two events from St. Joseph's life: the Annunciation to Joseph and the Birth of Jesus.

The Annunciation to Joseph Rosary Reflection

Background
In this Gospel story, Joseph becomes troubled by the news of Mary's unexpected pregnancy. God sends an Angel to reassure Joseph of God's plan to redeem Israel through her Son, Jesus.

God chose Mary to bear God's Son, yet she was vulnerable and needed the love, protection, and support of her husband during this time.

As a Dad, you can learn and adopt St. Joseph's example of following God's will. When you take the words of this Gospel passage to heart, you will be open to hear God speak to you, whether through a dream, a friend, or an angel. Trust that God is all-knowing, all-wise, and works out God's plan of saving others through your life and love, especially during your pregnancy.

The Annunciation to Joseph Reflection, according to the Gospel of Matthew, contains the full text of this marvelous story of God's action in his life.

First Decade: Joseph's Dilemma (Matthew 1:18-19)
This is how the birth of Jesus Christ came about. When his mother Mary was betrothed to Joseph, but before they lived together, she was found with child through the holy Spirit. Joseph, her husband, since he was a righteous man, yet unwilling to expose her to shame, decided to divorce her quietly.

Second Decade: The Angel's Appearance (Matthew 1:20)
Such was his intention when, behold, the angel of the Lord appeared to him in a dream and said, "Joseph, son of David, do not be afraid to take Mary your wife into your home."

Third Decade: Mary's Child (Matthew 1:21)
"For it is through the holy Spirit that this child has been conceived in her. She will bear a son and you are to name him, Jesus, because he will save his people from their sins."

Fourth Decade: Prophecy Fulfilled (Matthew 1:22-23)
All this took place to fulfill what the Lord had said through the prophet: "Behold, the virgin shall be with child and bear a son, and they shall name him Emmanuel," which means "God is with us."

Fifth Decade: Joseph Obeys God (Matthew 1:24-25)
When Joseph awoke, he did as the angel of the Lord had commanded him and took his wife into his home. He had no relations with her until she bore a son, and he named him Jesus.

What to Pray For

- For greater openness to hear God's messengers announcing God's plan to you during your pregnancy.
- For all expecting fathers and their commitment to love, protect, and support their expecting partners.
- For your personal intentions.

Pray the rosary using this Gospel for a deeper connection with St. Joseph, his love for God, and Mary's love and prayers for you.

The Birth of Jesus Rosary Reflection

Background

The second chapter of the Gospel of Luke tells the story of Jesus' birth. Mary and Joseph travel to Bethlehem to comply with a Roman decree for enrollment. While there, Mary gives birth to Jesus in a humble place, far away from the comfort of home in Nazareth.

This Gospel story shares the very beginning of Jesus' time on earth, even though He was born in humble circumstances. God became a human baby in Jesus, who needed the care and love of his mother and father.

God is at work in and through you to bring your child to birth, too, to experience your care and love as a father.

The Five Decades

Pray the Rosary in the usual way. When you pray the five decades of the Rosary, use these five moments from the Gospel story. Read the Gospel verses for each decade and let the words sink in as you pray that decade.

First Decade: Caesar Decrees an Enrollment (Luke 2:1-2)

In those day,s a decree went out from Caesar Augustus that the whole world should be enrolled. This was the first enrollment, when Quirinius was governor of Syria.

Second Decade: All People Comply With Caesar (Luke 2:3)

So all went to be enrolled, each to his own town.

Third Decade: Joseph and Mary Travel to Bethlehem (Luke 2:4-5)

And Joseph too went up from Galilee from the town of Nazareth to the city of David that is called Bethlehem, because he was of the house and family of David to be enrolled with Mary, his betrothed who was with child.

Fourth Decade: Mary Gives Birth (Luke 2:6-7a)

While they were there, the time came for her to have her child, and she gave birth to her first-born son.

Fifth Decade: Mary's Infant is Laid in a Manger (Luke 2:7b)

She wrapped him in swaddling clothes and laid him in a manger, because there was no room for them in the inn.

What to Pray For

- For a healthy delivery and birth for your partner, your baby, and your family.
- For all women who are giving birth, and the dads supporting them, especially those in poor countries and difficult life situations.
- For all medical doctors, nurses, and birth workers to have the grace and support to deliver babies safely.
- For your personal intentions.

Your Favorite Prayers

Feel free to list or write your favorite prayers in the space below.

Treasuring Scripture Passages

Both the Old Testament and the New Testament of the Bible contain many verses about the love God has for human beings. God treasures and loves every individual person. During your pregnancy, take time to think about how much God loves you, your partner, and your unborn child. Pray over them. Here are several verses to start with. Add your own favorites on the next page.

"Then God said, 'Let us make man in our image, after our likeness.' God created human beings in God's image; in the divine image God created him; male and female God created them. God looked at everything God had made and God found it very good." *Genesis 1: 26,27,31a*

"You will be a crown of splendor in the Lord's hand, a royal diadem in the hand of your God." *Isaiah 62:3*

"You are precious in my eyes and I love you." *Isaiah 43:4*

"You formed my inmost being; you knit me in my mother's womb. I praise you, so wonderfully you have made me; wonderful are your works!" *Psalm 139:13-14*

"I will give you treasures out of darkness, and riches that have been hidden, that you may know that I am the Lord, your God, who calls you by name." *Isaiah 45:3*

Jesus said: "As the Father loves me, I also love you. Remain in my love." *John 15:9*

"On that day the Lord of hosts will be a glorious crown and a brilliant diadem to the remnant of his people." Isaiah 28:5

"As a mother comforts her child, so will I comfort you." *Isaiah 66:13*

"Can a mother forget her infant, be without tenderness for the child of her womb? Even should she forget, I will never forget you. See, upon the palms of my hands I have written your name." *Isaiah 49:15-16a*

Your Favorite Scripture Verses

In the space below, write your favorite passages or verses from the Bible that you can speak to your partner and your baby. Come back to this list during your pregnancy and reflect on these words. Speak these words of love to your baby. Let yourself feel joyful about God's love for you, your family, and your baby.

Treasuring Words

Carrying Words of the Three Treasures

Like the Magi who carried and opened their treasures to give gifts to Jesus, you carry thoughts and words in your heart. You can open your mouth to speak those words. Your heart gives peace or stress, balance or uneasiness. Use this section to create a vocabulary and a strategy to keep the treasure and get rid of the trash.

A treasuring heart honors other people. Honoring involves deep respect. Jesus honored His Father and His disciples. Joseph and Mary honored each other. They praised God's work in their lives. As parents, they treasured their child Jesus–before and after birth.

This book has listed the three treasures God gives to honor every human being: the treasure of being, the treasure of doing, and the treasure of sharing. God's Word inspires life in you, your partner, and your baby.

Your words and support affect how your partner and you help your baby develop or hinder your baby from developing these three treasures during pregnancy. You have a choice to make.

Admire your partner and your baby's treasure of being. Encourage them to strengthen their treasures of doing. Appreciate your partner's connection to you and others.

Or you can destroy the trust, peace, love, and joy of your partner and your baby with negativity, ridicule, criticism, judgment, and belittling. What you give will come back to you. Belittling others makes you little by shrinking your heart. Don't go there!

Your partner and your baby need you to honor them during the pregnancy journey. Show your partner and your unborn child how much they mean to you by your treasuring words during this precious time.

Admiring Words to Honor the Treasure of Being

Admiring words are "wow!" messages. They express amazement at a person's traits and natural gifts given by God. Admiring messages are sentences that start with "You are…," like "You are growing. You are good. You are wonderful. You are beautiful. You are lovely." Another form of admiring words is Precious Gem for Your Partner Poems (page 108) and Precious Gem for Your Baby Poems (page 109.)

Admiring your partner is not flattery. Admiring acknowledges that she is made in God's Divine Image. All of a person's traits, natural abilities, and capacities are part of God's treasure of being to that person and to humanity. Every human being is created and called to be a unique person. God admires the work of God's hand and that includes you, your partner, and your baby! Imagine God holding you, your partner, and your baby like a diamond and admiring your beauty and brilliance. You *are*… in God's hands, mind, and heart.

Encouraging Words to Honor the Treasure of Doing

Encouraging words are "enabling" messages. They express confidence in your partner's ability to learn, develop skills, accomplish tasks, and achieve mastery. Encouraging messages are sentences that start with "You can…," like "You can move your arms. You can blink your eyes. You can turn over."

Encouraging your partner is not self-directed or for selfish purposes. Encouraging gives her courage, confidence, and heart. Your partner's abilities, talents, and skills are part of God's treasure of doing to her. Every human being is created and called to do good things in life. Jesus even told His disciples that they would do even greater works than He did.[21] God encourages every human being to grow and develop. That includes you, your partner, and your unborn child both before and after birth.

Appreciating Words to Honor the Treasure of Sharing

Appreciating words are about relationships. You share your presence with others and affirm their presence. These words tell how you connect, love, value, and treat others.Remember, the three persons in every relationship are you, another person, and God. Appreciating messages contain sentences that start with, "You mean, you count, you matter." Like "You mean the world to me," or "Your presence counts beyond what you can imagine," or "You matter to your family."

Appreciating your partner is not manipulating her to get her favor or her attention. Appreciation builds bonding, connection, and belonging. Your partner's capacities for giving and receiving love, respect, goodwill, and support are part of God's treasure of sharing with her. God prizes every human being as a valuable part of God's family. You, your partner, and your baby mean the world to God.

Precious Gem Poems for Your Partner

Do you remember the little Valentine's Day poems you wrote to someone when you were a kid? The poem starts "Roses are red and violets are blue, sugar is sweet and so are you!"

Precious gem poems are like that, except you use precious gems instead of flowers. Why? Because you and your partner are valuable and precious to God and to each other. Here are a few poems that you can write in your journal and read or sing aloud to your baby. Have fun. Make it joyful. Make up your own!

Rubies are red
And sapphires are blue:
I am so happy
To be always with you!

Rubies are red
And sapphires are blue:
I'm so in love
With the woman who is you!

Rubies are red
And sapphires are blue:
Our wonderful family
Starts with me and you.

Emeralds are green
And diamonds are white:
How giving you are,
You're shining God's light.

Diamonds are white
And rubies are red:
How lucky I am
That you're so well-bred.

Sapphires are blue
And emeralds are green:
How wonderful it is
To treat you like a queen.

Diamonds are white
And pearls do glow:
How amazing you are,
Much more than you know.

Rubies are red
And topaz is yellow:
Just being with you,
Makes me a happy fellow.

Sapphires are blue
And emeralds are green
When we met and right now,
I'm glad we're a team.

Diamonds are white
And sapphires are blue:
Whatever may come,
We'll see it through.

Pearls glow brightly
And diamonds do too
But they aren't as brilliant
As the woman that's you.

Rubies are gleaming,
And emeralds shine bright
Just be yourself
In you I delight!

Precious Gem Poems for Your Baby

More precious gem poems for your unborn child. Like the poems for your partner, these poems help you connect with your baby on a simple, deep, and emotional level.

You, your partner, and your baby are valuable and precious to God and to each other. Here are a few poems that you can write in your journal and read or sing aloud to your baby. Have fun. Make it joyful. Make up your own!

Rubies are red
And sapphires are blue:
God is so happy
To be always with you!

Rubies are red
And sapphires are blue:
I'm so amazed
At the beauty of you!

Rubies are red
And sapphires are blue:
How precious is
The treasure of you.

Emeralds are green
And diamonds are white:
How beautiful you are
Shining in God's light.

Diamonds are white
And rubies are red:
You're ready to sleep
When it's time for bed.

Sapphires are blue
And emeralds are green:
How pretty you are
Even though you're unseen.

Diamonds are white
And pearls do glow:
How lovely you are
And more as you grow.

Rubies are red
And emeralds are green:
The colors of Christmas,
Are in your genes.

Sapphires are blue
And emeralds are green
Mary's your mother
And a beautiful Queen.

Diamonds are white
And sapphires are blue:
Whatever may come,
We'll see it through.

Pearls glow brightly
And diamonds do too
But they aren't as brilliant
As the wonder of you.

Rubies are gleaming,
And emeralds shine bright
Just be yourself,
You are God's delight!

Your Favorite Poems or Sayings

In the space below, write your favorite poems or sayings that will inspire your partner or your baby. Come back to this list during your pregnancy and speak your words of love to them.

List of Beautiful, Loving Words

Use the words in this list when you talk to God, yourself, your partner, and your baby. In the left column, circle the words that feel right to you. Write your ideas in the middle column. Write down the favorite words of your partner in the right column. Then, say these words in simple sentences. The next several pages have several simple sentences you can say.

Suggested Words	Your Ideas	Her Favorites
Adorable		
Amazing		
Awesome		
Beautiful		
Beloved		
Breathtaking		
Charming		
Cherished		
Cute		
Darling		
Dazzling		
Delightful		
Dear to me		
Exquisite		
Extraordinary		
Fabulous		
Fantastic		
Gentle		
Gorgeous		
Graceful		
Incredible		
Lovely		
Loving		
Magnificent		
Marvelous		
Outstanding		
Precious		
Pretty		
Priceless		
Remarkable		
Sweet		
Sweetheart		
Terrific		
Tremendous		
Wonderful		

Admiring Sentences

Look at the list of beautiful, loving words on the previous page. Pick one word and use that word in one of these sentences. (Or make up your own sentence.) Write a sentence in your journal about what you treasure about yourself, your partner, and your unborn child. Then, read your words out loud. Use your name or your child's name. Smile as you speak the words!

Admiring Myself

__________, I think you are so ___________________!

Wow! How ______________ I am! Thank you God for making and loving me!

I am so happy because God made me _____________!

I look, feel, and believe that I am _________!

I love being __________!

I feel good about being_______.

I am made in God's likeness and Divine Image. I feel ________!

Admiring My Partner

__________, I think you are so ___________________!

Wow! You are so ___________! How blessed I am to live life with you.

I am so happy because God gave me such a(n) _________ partner!

When I think of you, it's so natural to think you are _______!

I think you are becoming a _________ mom for our baby.

You are ___________! Believe it–I do! I believe in you.

Admiring My Baby

I am so happy because you are ______________!

God is making you into a _________________ baby!

Mommy and I are so proud of you. You are _____________!

I am thanking and praising God that you are ____________!

You are growing to be ____________. I am so proud of you!

Encouraging Sentences

Encouraging sentences are simple sentences that affirm that you, your partner, and your baby can do or experience something. You can use these or make up your own.

Write down your sentence, then speak it out loud to yourself, your partner, and your baby.

Encouraging Myself

I can be present to my partner today.

I can become a loving dad and a more loving partner.

I can do what it takes to enjoy this special day of life for me, my family, and my baby.

I can take life one moment at a time.

I can give the love and support my partner needs today.

I can take the best care of my body so that my partner and baby feel safe and loved.

Encouraging My Partner

You are becoming the most wonderful mom to our baby.

You can make it through this pregnancy with flying colors.

Your love for our family makes our lives so precious.

You can get through this morning sickness and get better.

Your body is strong and and your love is stronger. I know this week will be an awesome time.

You can give birth to our baby as safely as possible.

I believe in you.

Encouraging My Baby

Your body can grow larger, stronger and healthier.

You can learn how to tell me what you need.

You can move your body with grace and ease.

You can sleep soundly and feel refreshed afterwards.

You can develop a healthy heart and lungs.

You can talk to God in your own special language.

Appreciating Sentences

Appreciating statements are simple sentences that let yourself, your partner, and your baby know how valuable each of you is. You can use these or make up your own.

Write down your words and sentences. Then speak them out loud to your loved ones!

Appreciating Myself

I am important to my partner, baby and my family.

I'm proud of the loving father I am becoming.

God is creating this wonderful new life, using our genes and love. We are so blessed.

I love myself. I love my partner. I love my baby. I love my family.

My life matters and I do too!

I mean the world to my baby and my family. God's love makes that happen.

Appreciating My Partner

You are so important to me and our growing family.

You mean the world to me and to our new baby!

Our baby is so blessed to have you as his/her Mom.

The world is a better place because you are alive and so is our family.

Your love and support mean so much more than I can tell. I can only say, "Thank you with all my heart."

I appreciate the big and little things you do for me. Thank you!

Thank you for being in my life!

Appreciating My Baby

I love spending time thinking about you.

God, Mom, and I love you no matter what.

I feel so lucky to be your dad.

I'm proud of the person you are becoming.

I thought of you today when I felt you (move, kick, smile.)

I'm grateful that you're in our lives and and inside Mom!

Nothing will ever make me stop loving you.

Treasuring Songs

Carry Your Family In Your Song

"The Lord your God is in your midst, a mighty savior; he will rejoice over you with gladness and renew you in his love, God will sing joyfully because of you, as one sings at festivals." Zephaniah 3:17-18a.

Your heart has a song for your family. Songs and music influence both your partner and your unborn child's and well-being. Songs bring courage, joy, hope, and tender love, especially to babies. Songs give hope. Your heart's song will give hope to your family.

In his ground-breaking book, *The Secret Life of the Unborn Child*,[22] Dr. Thomas Verny, M.D. wrote that certain types of music and songs are life-giving for unborn children. Gentle. Mild. Happy. Around the 24–27th week, babies can hear the outside world. They "hear" through their mother from very early on, from positive hormones like estrogen and oxytocin. Your baby is conscious and aware of its environment in your partner's womb.

Parents have sung to their babies for centuries. God sings to human beings. In his adult life, Jesus sang to God alone and with His disciples. Read the special verse in the Bible, from the Book of Zephaniah listed above. The prophet is speaking for God to discouraged people with a message that God loves and renews them. God sings to <u>you</u> as God's child every day and to your unborn child. And, at this book's beginning, Mary and St. Joseph sang a concert to you. Make sure to listen to those songs, at least one a day.

St. Joseph and Mary most likely sang to their unborn child, Jesus, when he was in Mary's womb. Moms of Mary's time sang to their babies. What would Mary sing to Jesus? Like her song of praise to God, the Magnificat, Mary would have sung of God's love, God's mercy, God's faithfulness, and God's protection. Mary's heart formed her baby Jesus' faith. Mary began the very life of God's Son, with a song of praise and joy in her heart, even when she faced the trials of daily living and uncertain times. Dads of St. Joseph's time sang to God in the synagogue and at home. St. Joseph knew Jesus' name before he was born. Speaking your baby's name is music to her ears.

Treasuring songs are treasuring words with music. Just like the section on *Treasuring Words*, treasuring songs contain words to admire, encourage, and appreciate your baby. Your sung words can help your baby grow its three treasures of being, doing, and sharing. Invite your partner to sing along with you, as a duet or in rounds. Don't worry; these songs are very simple. If you can sing "Old McDonald Had a Farm," you can sing these songs. Not only that, this book contains QR codes that you can scan with your mobile device. These QR codes link to the recorded songs you can play, hear and sing along.

Admiring Songs for the Treasure of Being
Tell your baby how amazing she/he is to value its treasure of being. Your baby is a unique person. He/she has a beautiful personality, gifts, and traits that will continue to grow throughout life.

Encouraging Songs for the Treasure of Doing
Sing these songs to inspire your baby to use its treasure of doing to grow during your pregnancy. Even though your child's body starts out as a cluster of cells, by the time your baby is born, she/he will have developed physically. Your baby's body, brain, and motion continue to grow after birth. You can sing encouraging songs as your baby moves and experiences its body.

Appreciating Songs for the Treasure of Sharing
These songs help your baby know what she/he means to you– and to God. Your baby feels wanted. Feeling wanted is a valuable part of belonging. You, your baby, family, friends and treasuring community belong to God's family. You can sing appreciating songs to teach your baby the value of sharing life together.

Preparing for Birth Songs
During the last few weeks of pregnancy, your baby is getting ready for birth. Childbirth may be a struggle for you and your baby. You can help your baby prepare for birth by offering songs of moving onward and being face-to-face with you.

Birth Songs and Newborn Songs
Giving birth takes effort, focus, and endurance. Having a birth song to sing can help you frame the birth experience as a welcome to new life. You can help yourself and your baby endure a birth process with a song on your lips and music in your heart. Continue singing to your baby after birth to treasure your new life together. You can bond more deeply with your baby.

The following pages have songs to sing to your unborn child. The melodies come from popular nursery rhymes and children's songs. Scan the QR code with your mobile device, and tap the SoundCloud link to play and hear a recorded version.

The *Treasuring Action Pages* section will suggest the songs you can sing to your unborn child during a specific week of pregnancy.

Admiring Songs

Song Lyrics

Song Title: It's a New Day to Rise and Shine

Tune: The Wheels on the Bus

Song Type: Admiring Song

Why Sing This Song?

Help your baby admire his/her treasure of being with God's love, hope, and joy in a new day through you!

Words to Sing:

It's a new day to rise and shine
Rise and shine, rise and shine.
It's a new day for the Son to shine,
Shining with God's love.

It's a new day to sing a song,
Sing a song, sing a song.
It's a new day to sing along,
The hope God sings to you.

It's a new day to laugh and play
Laugh and play, laugh and play.
It's a new day to smile away,
How wondrous are you made.

It's a new day that's filled with love
Filled with love, filled with love.
It's a new day that's full of love,
The love God has for you.

Song Lyrics

Song Title: Mommy Has a Precious One

Tune: Mary Had a Little Lamb

Song Type: Admiring Song

Why Sing This Song?

Sing this song to let your baby know how precious she/he is to you and God.

Words to Sing:

Mommy has a precious one,
Precious one, precious one.
Mommy has a precious one.
That God has helped to make.

Mom carries her precious one,
Precious one, precious one.
Mom carries her precious one,
You are her precious one.

Jesus loves mom's precious one,
Precious one, precious one.
Jesus loves mom's precious one,
To share His wondrous light.

Song Lyrics

Song Title: Oh My Baby

Tune: Baa, Baa, Black Sheep

Song Type: Admiring

Why Sing This Song?

Sing this little daily affirmation to let your baby know you love him/her.

Words to Sing:

Oh my baby
How is life today?
Mommy loves you
In ev'ry way.

You are so precious
My little gem
You are a diamond
shining from within.

Lovely baby
I just want to say
You're my darling
I love you today.

Song Lyrics

Song Title: Shining, Glowing, Little One

Tune: Twinkle, Twinkle Little Star

Song Type: Admiring Song

Why Sing This Song?

Affirm your unborn child shining out in the darkness of your womb, a precious jewel.

Words to Sing:

Shining, glowing, little one:
You're so precious, like the sun.

Growing bigger every day,
Lighting all up in your way.

Shining, glowing, little one:
You're so precious, like the sun.

Song Lyrics

Song Title: Sleep Little Baby

Tune: Hush Little Baby

Song Type: Admiring Song

Why Sing This Song?

Teach your baby about the love, joy, and happiness God wants your baby to have now and forever.

Words to Sing:

Sleep little baby
Don't make a sound
God's gonna make you
A royal crown.

And when that royal
Crown is made,
God's gonna weave
Your body braid.

And when your body
Glows at night
God's gonna fill
Your soul with light.

And when your soul
Is filled with glee,
God's gonna give you
a family.

And when your family
Gathers near
God's gonna have them
Raise a cheer.

And when they cheer you
with their voice.
God's gonna make us
All rejoice.

Song Lyrics

Song Title: Jesus Loves You

Tune: Alouette (French song)

Song Type: Admiring Song

Why Sing This Song?

Encourage your unborn child to grow and feel God's love through you!

Words to Sing:

Jesus loves you
Yes, He really loves you,
Jesus loves you,
With all of His Heart.
Jesus loves you,
Yes He really loves you,
Jesus loves you,
Wondrous work of art.
Now, He loves you through and through
Now His love is always true
He's with you,
Makes you new.
Jesus loves you,
With all of His Heart.
Jesus loves you,
Wondrous work of art

Mary loves you
Yes, she really loves you,
Mary loves you,
With all of her heart.
Mary loves you,
Yes she really loves you,
Mary loves you,
you are her sweetheart.
Now, she loves you ev'ry day,
A mom who will always pray,
Day by day,
She will stay.
Mary loves you,
With all of her heart.
Mary loves you,
you are her sweetheart.

Song Lyrics

Song Title: My Precious Little Darling

Tune: Itsy Bitsy Spider

Song Type: Admiring Song

Why Sing This Song?

Tell your baby how precious he/she is and that life will get better after birth.

Words to Sing:

My precious, little darling
You're glowing in the dark
Growing and floating
Just like Noah's Ark.
Soon, you'll come out
And be dancing in the sun,
Then, my precious, little darling
You'll learn to walk and run.

Song Lyrics

Song Title: You're My Little Pearl

Tune: I'm a Little Teapot

Song Type: Admiring Song

Why Sing This Song?

Show your baby it is okay to move, kick, and then relax.

Words to Sing:

You're my little pearl
Gleaming bright
Alive at every moment
Day and night
When you start kicking, I feel tight,
Relax your heart and make me right.

Encouraging Songs

Song Lyrics

Song Title: Glow, Glow, Glow and Float

Tune: Row, Row, Row Your Boat

Song Type: Encouraging Song

Why Sing This Song?

Very early in your pregnancy, you baby is floating inside you. This song encourages her/him to glow.

Words to Sing:

Glow, glow, glow, and float
Every day you start.
Shining, gleaming, inside mommy:
A diamond dancing in my heart.

Song Lyrics

Song Title: Hair and Teeth Are Growing Now

Tune: London Bridge is Falling Down

Song Type: Encouraging Song

Why Sing This Song?

Sing this song to encourage your baby to develop as she/he grows inside you.

Words to Sing:

(Weeks 16+)

Taste and ears are working now
Working now, working now
Taste and ears are working now
My fine baby.

(Weeks 19+)

Hair and teeth are growing now
Growing now, growing now
Your hair and teeth are growing now,
My fine baby.

(Weeks 24+)

Heart and lungs are working now
Working now, working now.
Heart and lungs are working now
My fine baby.

(Week 35+)

Brain and nerves grow rapidly.
Rapidly, rapidly.
Brain and nerves grow rapidly.
My fine baby.

(Feel free to make up your own verses to this simple melody.)

Song Lyrics

Song Title: Joyfully You Grow Today

Tune: Merrily We Roll Along

Song Type: Encouraging Song

Why Sing This Song?

Sing this song to encourage your baby to be happy to grow and develop inside you today.

Words to Sing:

Joyfully, you grow today
Grow today, grow today.
Joyfully, you grow today,
God is loving you.

Healthily, you live today,
Live today, live today,
Healthily, you live today,
God's life flows in you.

Gratefully, I carry you,
Carry you, carry you.
Gratefully, I carry you:
God's love carries us.

(Feel free to make up your own verses to this simple melody.)

Song Lyrics

Song Title: My Baby's Lungs

Tune: The Wheels on the Bus

Song Type: Encouraging Song

Why Sing This Song?

Affirm your baby's efforts to move and use his/her body during pregnancy.

Words to Sing:

My baby's face
Shines in God's love
In God's love,
in God's love
My baby's face
Shines with God's love
All through the day.

(Weeks 5+)

My baby's body
Rests and naps,
Rests and naps,
rests and naps
My baby's body
Rests and naps,
All through the day

(Weeks 18+)

My baby moves
With grace and ease
In God's ease,
in God's peace
My baby moves
With grace and ease
All through the day.

(Weeks 22+)

My baby's lungs
Breathe in and out,
In and out,
in and out,
My baby's lungs
Breathe in and out,
All through the day.

(Week 24, 27)

My baby's nose
Smells lots of things
Lots of things,
lots of things.
My baby's nose
Smells lots of things
All through the day.

(Week 25)

My baby's heart
Beats healthily
Healthily, healthily
My baby's heart
Beats healthily
All through the day.

(Week 37)

Song Lyrics

Song Title: My Precious One is In God's Heart

Tune: This Old Man

Song Type: Encouraging Song

Why Sing This Song?

Sing this song about your baby's progressive growth and how lovely and beloved she/he is.

Words to Sing:

My precious one, in month two
She/he grows bigger in my womb
As a Lovely, Beloved,
Wondrous work of art,
My precious one is in God's heart.

(Weeks 8-11)

My precious one, in month three,
Floating now and swimming free
As a Lovely, Beloved
Wondrous work of art,
My precious one is in God's heart.

(Weeks 12-15)

My precious one, in month four
Waking up and sleeping more
As a Lovely, Beloved,
Wondrous work of art,
My precious one is in God's heart.

(Weeks 16-19)

My precious one, in month five
I'm so grateful you're alive.
As a Lovely, Beloved,
Wondrous work of art,
My precious one is in God's heart.

(Weeks 20-23)

Song Lyrics

Song Title: My Precious One is in God's Heart

Tune: This Old Man

Song Type: Encouraging Song

Why Sing This Song?

Sing this song about your baby's progressive growth and how lovely and beloved she/he is.

(Weeks 24-27)

My precious one, in month six
You're the first one of my picks
As a Lovely, Beloved,
Wondrous work of art,
My precious one is in God's heart.

(Weeks 28-32)

My precious one, in month seven
Angels guard now from heaven
As a Lovely, Beloved,
Wondrous work of art,
My precious one is in God's heart.

(Weeks 32-25)

My precious one, in month eight
Dreams of things small and great
As a Lovely, Beloved,
Wondrous work of art,
My precious one is in God's heart.

(Weeks 36-40)

My precious one, in month nine
Waits to be born and to shine
As a Lovely, Beloved,
Wondrous work of art,
My precious one is in God's heart.

Song Lyrics

Song Title: Precious Baby, Start to Grow Today

Tune: Old MacDonald

Song Type: Encouraging Song

Why Sing This Song?

Encourage your baby to feel, move, and love his/her growing body during his/her time in your womb.

Words to Sing:

Precious baby, move your legs.
Start to grow today.
And with your legs, swing them free
Start to grow today.
With tissues here, tissues there
Here a tissue, there a tissue
Everywhere grow your tissues.
Precious baby, move your legs
Start to grow today.

(Weeks 15+)

Precious baby, learn to eat
Start to grow today.
Swallow, digest, eat your fill.
Start to grow today.
With a swallow here
Digesting there,
Here a swallow, There a swallow,
Your tummy isn't hollow
Precious baby, learn to eat.
Start to grow today,

(Weeks 21, 33+)

Song Lyrics

Song Title: Precious Baby, Start to Grow Today

Tune: Old MacDonald

Song Type: Encouraging Song

Why Sing This Song?

Encourage your baby to feel, move, and love his/her growing body during his/her time in your womb.

(Weeks 22+)

Precious baby, move your hands.
Start to grow today.
And with your hands, swing them free
Start to grow today.
With clapping here, clapping there
Here a clap, there a clap
Everywhere you're clapping.
Precious baby, move your hands
Start to grow today.

(Weeks 27+)

Precious baby, use your lungs
Start to grow today.
And with your lungs,
practice breath
Start to grow today.
With an inhale here, an exhale there
Here inhaling,
there exhaling
It's so exhilarating.
Precious baby, use your lungs,
Start to grow today.

Song Lyrics

Song Title: Precious Baby, Start to Grow Today

Tune: Old MacDonald

Song Type: Encouraging song

Why Sing This Song?

Encourage your baby to feel, move, and love his/her growing body during his/her time in your womb.

Precious baby, blink your eyes.
Start to grow today.
And with your eyes, Look to see.
Start to grow today.
With colors here, colors there
Here a color, there a color,
Everywhere see your colors
Precious baby,
blink your eyes.
Start to grow today.

(Week 28)

Precious baby, wiggle toes.
Start to grow today.
And with your toes,
Glide to dance.
Start to grow today.
With a two-step here,
A two-step there
Here a step, there a step
Everywhere dance your steps.
Precious baby, wiggle toes,
Start to grow today.

(Weeks 34+)

Song Lyrics

Song Title: At Two Months Now

Tune: Three Blind Mice

Song Type: Encouraging Song

Why Sing This Song?

Encourage and affirm your baby's ongoing growth during each month of your pregnancy.

Words to Sing:

At two months now,
At two months now.
See how you've grown, see how you've grown
Your body gets stronger every day, God's love for you is deeper every day
You're fearfully, wondrously made at two months now.

2 months
8-11 weeks

3 months
12-15 weeks

4 months
16-19 weeks

5 months
20-23 weeks

6 months
25-28 weeks

7 months
29-32 weeks

8 months
33-36 weeks

9 months
37-40 weeks

Appreciating Songs

Song Lyrics

Song Title: Do You Love My Baby Dear?

Tune: Do You Know the Muffin Man?

Song Type: Appreciating Song

Why Sing This Song?

This is a family song to sing together to let your unborn baby know that you love him/her.

Words to Sing:

Oh, do you love my baby dear?
My baby dear, my baby dear.
Oh, do you love my baby dear,
Who lives, my precious one?

Oh, yes we love our baby dear,
Our baby dear, our baby dear.
Oh, yes we love our baby dear.
Who lives, our precious one.

Oh, we all love our baby dear,
Our baby dear, our baby dear.
Oh, we all love our baby dear.
Who lives, our precious one.

Song Lyrics

Song Title: God is Knitting

Tune: Frère Jacques (Are You Sleeping?)

Song Type: Appreciating Song

Why Sing This Song?

Teach your baby that God loves and helps him/her to grow during the time in your womb.

Words to Sing:

God is knitting
God is knitting
Loving you
All of you.
God sings a love song to you
God brings a love song to you
Every day,
Every day.

God is quilting
God is quilting
Covering you
Covering you
Rest in God's protection
Sleep in my midsection
God treasures you
And I do too.

God is loving
God is loving
All of you
All the time.
Yes, you are so lovely.
Yes, you are so loving.
Made of love,
Grow in love.

I am loving,
I am loving
All of you,
All the time.
You are my little darling
My precious little darling
I love you.
I love you.

Song Lyrics

Song Title: God Makes You So Shining New

Tune: Jack and Jill Went Up a Hill

Song Type: Appreciating Song

Why Sing This Song?

Sing these simple words of hope about God's love and presence with him/her every day.

Words to Sing:

God makes you
So shining new
To share a life together.
When you're born,
Both night and morn,
God lives with you forever.

Song Lyrics

Song Title: In Your Sacred Space

Tune: Pop Goes the Weasel

Song Type: Appreciating Song

Why Sing This Song?

Encourage your baby to feel safe as she/he grows bigger each day within you.

Words to Sing

In your sacred space inside of me
You're safe and warm, my baby.
Dance and sing, play inside of me
"Yes!" says the baby!

A little bigger every day
A little better too.
Loved by God, dad and me:
"Yes!" says the baby!

Song Lyrics

Song Title: You Are Wonderfully Made

Tune: Original

Song Type: Appreciating Song

Why Sing This Song?

A happy song that affirms your baby's body, mind, emotions and soul. (And a song to sing to yourself!)

Words to Sing:

You are fearfully and wonderfully made.
You are fearfully and wonderfully made.
So, when you are dismayed,
Or when you feel afraid,
Please recall in you God's glory is displayed.

There is only one and only one of you.
There is only one and only one of you.
So, God made you brand new,
To be the grand you,
Be glad that God's love is alive in you.

I am fearfully and wonderfully made.
I am fearfully and wonderfully made.
So, when I am dismayed,
Or when I feel afraid,
I recall in you God's glory is displayed.

There is only one and only one of me.
There is only one and only one of me.
So, God created me
To love and be set free
I am glad God's love is alive in me.

Song Lyrics

Song Title: Loving You, Loving You

Tune: Pat-A-Cake, Pat-A-Cake

Song Type: Appreciating Song

Why Sing This Song?

Teach your baby how much you and God love and want him/her to grow.

Words to Sing:

Loving you, loving you,
all we can.
Keep on growing
As long as you can.

Smiling and crying
Everything is good
God's love fills you
All your childhood.

Loving you, loving you,
all we can.
Keep on learning
As much as you can.

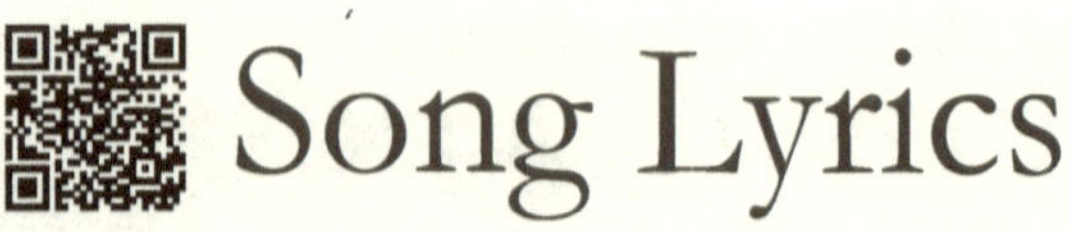

Song Title: Sleep Now My Baby

Tune: Rock a Bye Baby

Song Type: Appreciating Song

Why Sing This Song?

Use this quiet lullaby to encourage your baby to rest and be at peace now.

Words to Sing:

Sleep now my baby
God is your shade
In God's Divine Image
You are well made.

When you are born
That Image will shine
For then my dear baby
You will be mine.

Song Lyrics

Song Title: There's a Loving God

Tune: B-I-N-G-O

Song Type: Appreciating Song

Why Sing This Song?

Teach your baby the names of Jesus, Mary and Joseph, whose love is with your baby always.

Words to Sing:

There's a loving God
Who sent His Son
And Jesus is His Name-o
J-E-S-U-S
J-E-S-U-S
J-E-S-U-S
And Jesus is His Name-o

There's a loving mom
Who sings to you
And Mary is her name-o
M-A-R-I-A
M-A-R-I-A
M-A-R-I-A
And Mary is her name-o.

There's a loving dad
Who prays for you
And Joseph is his name-o
S-T-J-O-E
S-T-J-O-E
S-T-J-O-E
And Joseph is his name-o.

Preparing for Birth Songs

Song Lyrics

Song Title: It's a New Day to Rest and Turn

Tune: The Wheels on the Bus

Song Type: Preparing for Birth Song

Why Sing This Song?

Encourage your baby to prepare for birth by turning, resting, and breathing.

Words to Sing:

It's a new day to rest and turn.
Rest and turn, rest and turn.
It's a new day for you to learn,
God wants you to be born.

It's a new day to rest and breathe.
Rest and breathe, rest and breathe.
It's a new day to breathe with me.
You'll be breathing when you're born.

It's a new day to rest and eat.
Rest and eat. Rest and eat.
It's a new day to rest and eat.
You'll eat with me when you're born.

It's a new day that's filled with love
Filled with love, filled with love.
It's a new day that's full of love,
The love God has for you.

Song Lyrics

Song Title: A Few Weeks Now

Tune: Three Blind Mice

Song Type: Preparing for Birth Song

Why Sing This Song?

Let your baby know God and you are waiting to see him/her face-to-face at birth.

Words to Sing:

A few weeks now, a few weeks now.
You'll see a new day. You'll see a new day.
Your body gets stronger every day
God's love is bringing you face-to-face.
You'll be coming home to live with us,
A few weeks now.

As your due date approaches, change the words, "A few weeks now" in the first and last lines to:

Any day now….

Any time now…

Song Lyrics

Song Title: God is Bringing You to Birth

Tune: Frère Jacques (Are You Sleeping?)

Song Type: Preparing for Birth Song

Why Sing This Song?

Teach your baby that you are waiting to welcome your baby and waiting to see him/her face-to-face.

Words to Sing:

God is bringing
God is bringing
You to birth.
A new birth.
God sings a love song to you
God brings a love song to you
When you're born
You'll be born.

I am waiting,
I am waiting.
Looking for you,
Waiting for you.
So much love is waiting,
So much joy is waiting.
To see you.
To see you.

Birth Songs

Song Lyrics

Song Title: Your Little Head is Coming Out

Tune: London Bridge is Falling Down

Song Type: Birth Song

Why Sing This Song?

Sing this song to encourage your baby to come out of your womb, a little at a time.

Words to Sing:

Your little head is coming out
Coming out, coming out.
Your little head is coming out,
My fine baby.

Your little body's coming out
Coming out, coming out.
Your little body's is coming out,
My fine baby.

Your little feet are coming out
Coming out, coming out.
Your little feet are coming out,
My fine baby.

(Feel free to make up your own verses to this simple melody.)

Song Lyrics

Song Title: My Baby's Born

Tune: The Wheels on the Bus

Song Type: Birth Song

Why Sing This Song?

Encourage your baby to be healthy during and after birth.

Words to Sing:

My baby's born
To us today
Us today, us today
My baby's born
Coming out all the way,
Welcome to you!

My baby's heart
Beats healthily
Healthily, healthily
My baby's heart
Beats healthily
Welcome to you!

My baby moves
With grace and ease
Grace and ease, grace and ease
My baby moves
With grace and ease
Welcome to you!

My baby's face
Shines with God's love
With God's love, with God's love
My baby's face
Shines with God's love
We love you so.

Song Lyrics

Song Title: Happy Birth Day to You

Tune: Happy Birthday to You

Song Type: Birth Song

Why Sing This Song?

Sing this song to celebrate your baby's birth day, the very first day living with you face-to-face.

Words to Sing:

Happy Birth Day to you,
Happy Birth Day to you,
Happy Birth Day, dear [your baby's name].
Happy Birth Day to you!

I'm so glad you're here,
I'm so glad you're here,
I'm so glad you're with us,
I'm so glad you're here.

God loves you so much.
God loves you so much
God loves you, dear [your baby's name]
God loves you so much.

(Feel free to make up your own verses to this simple melody.)

Newborn Songs

Song Lyrics

Song Title: Do You See My Baby Dear?

Tune: Do You Know the Muffin Man?

Why Sing This Song?

This is a family song to sing together to let your newborn baby know that you love him/her.

Words to Sing:

Oh, do you see my baby dear?
My baby dear, my baby dear.
Oh, do you see my baby dear,
Who came to live with us?

Oh, yes we see our baby dear,
Our baby dear, our baby dear.
Oh, yes we see our baby dear.
Who came to live with us.

Oh, we all love our baby dear,
Our baby dear, our baby dear.
Oh, we all love our baby dear.
Who came to live with us.

Song Lyrics

Song Title: God Makes You So Wonderful

Tune: Jack and Jill Went Up a Hill

Why Sing This Song?

Sing these simple words of hope about God's love and presence with him/her every day.

Words to Sing:

God made you
So wonderful
To share a life together.
Now you're born,
Both night and morn,
God lives with us forever.

Composing Your Songs

You may have a song in your mind and a dream in your heart for your baby's health and well-being during your pregnancy. You may have a favorite song or two that inspires you, help you feel at peace, and fill your heart with awe and wonder. Or you may get creative. When you listen to a popular tune or a song, other words to affirm your partner and your baby just come to mind.

That is a gift. Write those words down. Experiment with a melody. Don't be afraid to revise the words for a better message for your child. Then, sing them to your partner and your baby.

A word of wisdom: compose and sing songs that will honor your family to grow. The messages that you give your baby will affect its growth. Use words that are life-giving. Words that admire your baby, encourage your baby and appreciate your baby's presence inside you. Songs of peace. Songs of love. Healthy babies need to feel loved and wanted by their fathers and mothers. God wants you and your baby to be happy together–forever.

Use the following pages to write your song that will help your baby feel your love and care. What wonderful words of your own can you sing to honor your unborn child?

<u>Child of Wonder</u> *(Note from the composer)*

When my wife was expecting our first child, I composed a song for her that I titled *Child of Wonder*. Here are those lyrics:

> *<u>Refrain:</u> You're a child of wonder, the splendor of a dream, that our God has sung forever, the gift of family.*
>
> You're the dust of a star, created from God's light, glowing in the darkness. Radiance in bloom, shine in mommy's womb. *Refrain.*
>
> You're the seed of a song, with notes that no one can hear, composed in the darkness, holy sound arise, sing in daddy's eyes. *Refrain.*
>
> You're the sigh of a breath from the Spirit paused at rest, knitting in the darkness, work of wondrous art, weave in Abba's heart. *Refrain.*
>
> You're the hope of a world that waits upon your birth dancing in the darkness. Let all the earth rejoice: live in Jesus' voice. *Refrain.*

Song Lyrics

Song Title:

Tune: Tune:

Song Type:

Why Sing This Song?

Words to Sing:

Song Lyrics

Song Title:

Tune: Tune:

Song Type:

Why Sing This Song?

Words to Sing:

Song Lyrics

Song Title:

Tune: Tune:

Song Type:

Why Sing This Song?

Words to Sing:

Treasuring Action Pages

Carrying Out Your Legacy of Love

Your *Treasuring Action Pages* help you create a treasury of precious moments and positive memories during your pregnancy journey. The following pages are a resource for you to plan how to treasure your partner and your baby, as well as write out what you experience during your pregnancy journey. There are enough pages to cover each week, starting with week 5 through week 40 of your pregnancy.

You can plan treasuring actions each week. A normal pregnancy may last 40 weeks; your length of pregnancy may be shorter or longer. Your baby may develop faster or slower than the common experience of pregnancy. Stay present about what is happening with your partner and check in with her doctor's advice.

The First Four Weeks

You won't be aware of your pregnancy until your partner misses a menstrual period. She may take a pregnancy test then or have an ultrasound to verify your baby's presence. God is already creating your child from conception through the first four weeks. The first section[23] of these pages includes *Weeks 1–4*, which outlines how God is working through your partner during this time. Make sure to read these pages to understand the wonderful work God is doing in creating your baby.

Weekly Introduction Page

Starting with Week 5, each treasuring action section has four pages. The first page is the introductory page with the name of the week, a summary of the typical growth that your baby experiences, and what your partner might experience during this time. Read this page to be aware of what your partner and your baby might be experiencing. This is the Listen and Observe part of the LOVE Compass. Around Week 32 (or sooner), you will need to get your baby's living space ready after birth.

The top right corner of the Weekly Introduction Page features a QR code that links to a video describing a treasuring plan for that link. Use the camera of your mobile device to scan the QR code and play the video.

Weekly Treasuring Plan Page

The second page of your weekly treasuring action pages is your action plan for your partner and your baby. This is where you plan to give practical love to them. This page helps to you remember to ask St. Joseph to help you love your partner and baby: kind, patient, gentle, soft-hearted, thoughtful, self-giving. The three treasuring attitudes are listed here as a reminder: appreciate, encourage, and admire. Pick the song(s) from Mary and Joseph on pages 14-45 you want to hear, to reinforce a positive view of fathering.

For Your Partner
The top section of your Treasuring Plan is a place where you can write what you want to do to make your partner feel loved this week.

Read the section on *What Your Partner Might Experience* so that you have an awareness of what she is going through. She needs your love and support, especially when she feels the aches and pains of pregnancy, the emotional ups and downs, and other changes to her body.

Decide which of the five composing actions you want to share with her. (See pages 111-114 for your lists.) The more ways that you show your love to her, the better. Ask your partner what she needs and wants at the moment, then give it to her.

For Your Baby
List the songs you plan to sing to your unborn child, the words you want to say, and the topics you want to talk to your baby about. Focus on the attributes of love you want to live.

You can talk to your baby about anything, especially what your baby might experience that day or that week. Put your hand on your partner's belly when you talk. You can talk about what you are experiencing: how lovely your partner is, your day at work, how excited you are to have your baby in your life, and so much more. Your baby will "hear" your voice in his/her heart through your partner's good feelings when she hears you talking to your baby. Around Week 24, your baby hears your voice with her/his ears. She/he is connected to you in body, heart, mind, and soul. After birth, your baby will recognize your voice because you spoke to her before she was born.

Use the blank space in the Treasuring Words section of the Treasuring Plan to write a word or sentence that you want to say to your baby.

Choose the Admiring and Appreciating Songs you want to sing to your baby for the week. There is one or more Encouraging Songs suggested that aligns with your baby's expected growth for that week.

In the *Topics to Tell Baby* area, write what you want to talk to your baby about. You may wish to tell your baby how he/she may grow this week. Use the information in *Your Baby Grows This Week* to encourage and praise your child.

Weekly Journal Pages

There are two journal pages that follow the Weekly Treasuring Plan page. These pages contain contains several blank lines under four sections: I Treasure God, I Treasure My Partner, I Treasure My Unborn Baby and I Treasure Me. In the space provided at the top of the page, write the date at the top of the page. Remember, you are starting a new habit, so start tiny. (See page 52.)

I Treasure God

Find a quiet spot, close your eyes, and get in touch with God's love that is present in you. Think of how marvelous it is for God to create this special, tiny person right inside of you. An awesome God who has plans of hope and wonder for you, your child, and your family. A precious little diamond that God wants to sparkle with beauty for all eternity with God and you.

Now, use the *I Treasure God* area to write a few words, one sentence, or your thoughts to God about the special things that are happening this day with your baby, within you, and within your family.

Ask God for help, protection, safety, and health; praise God for this marvelous gift of creation happening inside of your partner. Write God a love note for the day. Get started now and after you write your journal entry, read it out loud. Let yourself feel the joy, peace, and love that God has, especially for your partner, your child, you, and your family.

I Treasure My Partner

Write the admiring, encouraging, and appreciating words and sentences to your partner. During your pregnancy, she needs to know that she is LOVEd: you admire, encourage and appreciate her, what she is going through during this pregnancy. Her presence is wanted, and the baby is important to you. Your love and support for her and your baby are essential now, and after your baby is born. Make her feel your love.

I Treasure My Unborn Baby
Go to this section and write a little love note to your unborn child, something you experienced or did today. If you have chosen your baby's name, write his/her name in your note. If you sang a treasuring song to your baby, write the title of it. If you spoke some treasuring words to your baby, write that sentence.

Your child is a special gift, like a precious diamond or a lovely pearl growing inside of your partner. Let your unborn baby feel your love and joy.

Honor your child by writing beautiful, loving words or singing a treasuring song. Use admiring, encouraging, and appreciating sentences. Read or sing those words out loud to your child.

Let yourself feel good about working together with God and your partner to bring the beautiful child inside of your partner to birth.

I Treasure Me
Go to the *I Treasure Me* area and write yourself a note of admiration, encouragement, or appreciation. You are present to your partner and your baby. You have fathered a special child growing within your partner. You have a God who loves you more than you can imagine. Remember, there are many other people, whom you can't even see, who are praying for you.

Honor yourself with kind words. Use admiring, encouraging, and appreciating sentences. Think of the good things you have in life. Let yourself feel good about being the marvelous man you are and the fantastic father you are becoming. Remember, the more positive you feel about yourself, the more your partner and your baby will absorb your "good vibes."

Sample Pages
The next three pages include a sample Treasuring Plan and journal pages to give you a picture of what the following sections can look like. Your own Treasuring Plans and journaling will be what you make them to be.

Sample Treasuring Plan: Week 28

Each day this week, St. Joseph help me to be:

Loving • Joyful • Peaceful • Patient • Kind • Generous • Faithful • Gentle • Self-Controlled

Strategy: Admire • Encourage • Appreciate

The Mary/St. Joseph songs I will listen to this week:	*A Father's Legacy*

For My Partner (Sue)

The Music I Am Making	What I Am Doing	Done
Finding the Melody (page 37)	Massage Sue's feet and legs when she feels swelling and cramps. Hug Sue twice a day.	√
Writing Treasuring Lyrics (page 38)	Say, "I love you, Sue!" and "You are such a wonderful mom!" at least three times a day.	√
Making Notation (page 39)	Give Sue a daisy on Wednesday.	√
Rehearsing Your Love (page 40)	Cook Sue's favorite fish taco dinner. Clean toilets, vacuum, car oil change.	√
Performing in Person (page 41)	Do resting prayer with Sue and Charlie each day at 7:00 pm.	√

For My Unborn Baby (Charlie)

Affirming Action	What I Am Doing	Done
Treasuring Words	Charlie is a healthy, wonderful boy who is my little guy.	√
Admiring Songs	Check with Sue and sing with her.	√
Encouraging Songs	Since Charlie is using his eyes more, "Precious Baby, Blink Your Eyes" (p 67)	√
Appreciating Songs	Check with Sue and sing with her.	√
Topics to Tell Baby	My day at work, how his room is coming along, how great Sue sews and quilts.	√

Weekly Journal

Dates: ________________

I Treasure God

Dear God, Thank you for this week. I am so grateful for Sue's health and Charlie's growth inside her. It is such a marvelous thing to think about–Charlie is using his eyes to move around and blink. There are so many beautiful things to see in this world . You made them all–canyons, forests, trees, the sunrise and stars. My heart is so full of thanks that Charlie will have so much wonder to look forward to and behold.

I love you, Bill

I Treasure My Partner

Dear Sue, I love and treasure you! The quilt you are making for Charlie is so beautiful! You have such a creative gift, I imagine how beautiful Charlie will be when he's born–you're making a wondrous work of art with God's guidance. My love grows deeper for you every day and I am so glad God is giving us this child for our family. I don't know if I ever you–I've dreamed of having a son since our third date and now that dream is coming true. You will be the best mom ever! Love always, Bill

"You formed my inmost being; you knit me in my mother's womb. I praise you, so wonderfully you have made me; wonderful are your works!" Psalm 139:13-14

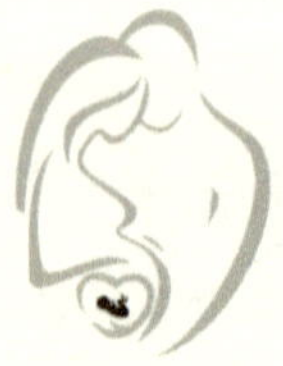

Weekly Journal

Dates: ________________

I Treasure My Unborn Baby

Dear Charlie, I love and treasure you! What a wonderful boy you are. I am so happy to learn you are blinking your eyes now as your body keeps growing inside Mommy. There are so many beautiful things to see in this world. Your eyes will see them, God, Mommy, and I have so many things to show you. Just wait and see. You are my best boy ever.

Love, Daddy

I Treasure Me

Dear Bill, I treasure you! When I look back at the first day I learned we were expecting, I can't believe how much you've grown as a father. And you haven't even held your son yet! You have become more patient and more understanding with Sue. You actually sang the "Old MacDonald Songs" and did resting prayer with Sue and Charlie. I believe you will grow even more loving as time goes on. I believe in you!

I love you, Bill. Your friend, Bill

Weeks 1–4

The Bible opens with the Book of Genesis. The Book of Genesis begins with two creation stories.[24] Chapter One depicts the all-powerful God speaking the words, *"Let there be…"* and different aspects of creation come into being. Chapter Two shows God intimately involved with shaping and forming the world, where God involves human beings.

God is still creating today. At this very moment, God is speaking and singing to creation. God shapes and forms creation through action. God involves you, especially in the conception, pregnancy, and birth of your child. Your parents did the same for you. Let the story of your baby's creation unfold during the nine months of pregnancy, as God whispers to your unborn baby in Mom's womb. You will witness the wonder of the God who formed you, and delight in your unborn child.

The Weekly Page uses the format of "*Then God whispers…*" in the *Your Baby Grows This Week* section to help you visualize God's creative action. The story of God's creation of your baby unfolds within you. Your baby's creation story starts at conception:

In your baby's beginning, there is a dark womb with a willing ovum waiting in mom's ovary, and a mass of dad's sperm cells cover the ovum.

Then God whispers, "Let there be life!" and there is life. God selects one of Dad's sperm cells and instructs the Mom's ovum to welcome the sperm cell inside. The two cells unite and your baby's body is conceived, and God gives your baby a soul. Your baby is alive. One second comes, and another second follows. Your baby's first moment.

Then God whispers, "Let this new baby become precious to Me." And so it happens. God molds your baby's soul to the Divine Image and Likeness and gives the three treasures of being, doing, and sharing upon your baby. God knits three strands of faith, love, and hope together to form the velvet lining of God's presence among those three treasures. A millisecond comes, and another millisecond follows. Your baby's precious moment.

Then God whispers, "Let this baby's tiny one-cell body multiply, divide, and travel to a new place that I will show it." And so it happens. The fertilized ovum divides once, then again, and again. That family of cells travels down Mom's Fallopian tube into her uterus and finds a place to live on her uterine wall. Your baby pitches a tent there and moves into a new home forming with a placenta. Four Sundays come, and four Saturdays follow, the first four weeks.

Week 5

Your Baby Grows This Week

Then God whispers, "Let the baby's body organize itself." And so it happens, your baby begins to develop a heart to pump blood and a neural tube for your baby's brain and nervous system. His/her cells separate into different body systems. An average baby is so tiny at this stage–only the size of a brush's bristle. Sunday comes and Saturday follows, the fifth week.

What Your Partner Might Experience This Week

At five weeks, expecting moms typically experience tender breasts, fatigue, nausea, frequent bathroom trips, and a range of emotions.

Use the LOVE Compass to listen to your partner and observe her emotions and stress levels. Then, form your treasuring plan so she can feel your love and care for her and your baby.

"Love one another as I have loved you." John 13:34

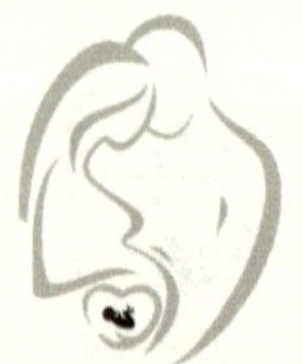

This Week's Treasuring Plan

Each day this week, St. Joseph help me to be:

Loving • Joyful • Peaceful • Patient • Kind • Generous • Faithful • Gentle • Self-Controlled

Strategy: Admire • Encourage • Appreciate

The Mary/St. Joseph songs I will listen to this week:	Any songs, pages 15-45

For My Life Partner

The Music I Am Making	What I Am Composing	Done
Daily Prayers	See pages 86-87.	
Finding Melody of Connection (Page 74)		
Writing Lyrics to Treasure (Page 75)		
Making Notation (Page 76)		
Rehearsing Your Love (Page 77)		
Performing in Person (Page 78)		

For My Unborn Baby

Affirming Action	What I Am Composing	Done
Daily Prayers	See pages 86-87.	
Words	See pages 111-114.	
Admiring Songs	Any song, pages 119-127.	
Encouraging Songs	Glow, glow, glow and float, page 129.	
Appreciating Songs	Any song, pages 139-147.	
Baby talk		

Weekly Journal

Dates: ________________

I Treasure God

I Treasure My Partner

"You formed my inmost being; you knit me in my mother's womb. I praise you, so wonderfully you have made me; wonderful are your works!" Psalm 139:13-14

Weekly Journal

Dates: ________________

I Treasure My Unborn Baby

____

____

____

____

____

____

____

____

____

I Treasure Me

____

____

____

____

____

____

____

____

____

Week 6

Your Baby Grows This Week

Then God whispers, "Let the baby form organs to support its body and limbs to move." And so it happens, your tiny baby's heart begins to beat. Your baby's face begins to grow a mouth, nostrils, ears, and eyes. Her/his legs and arms begin to sprout as buds from your baby's body. An average baby is about one-fourth inch long. Sunday comes and Saturday follows, the sixth week.

What Your Partner Might Experience This Week

At six weeks, expecting moms typically experience fatigue, morning sickness, and frequent urination. Her emotions may be up and down too.

Use the LOVE Compass to listen to your partner and observe her emotions and stress levels. Then, form your treasuring plan so she can feel your love and care for her and your baby.

"Love one another as I have loved you." John 13:34

This Week's Treasuring Plan

Each day this week, St. Joseph help me to be:

Loving • Joyful • Peaceful • Patient • Kind • Generous • Faithful • Gentle • Self-Controlled

Strategy: Admire • Encourage • Appreciate

The Mary/St. Joseph songs I will listen to this week:	Any songs, pages 15-45

For My Life Partner

The Music I Am Making	What I Am Composing	Done
Daily Prayers	See pages 86-87.	
Finding Melody of Connection (Page 74)		
Writing Lyrics to Treasure (Page 75)		
Making Notation (Page 76)		
Rehearsing Your Love (Page 77)		
Performing in Person (Page 78)		

For My Unborn Baby

Affirming Action	What I Am Composing	Done
Daily Prayers	See pages 86-87.	
Words	See pages 111-114.	
Admiring Songs	Any song, pages 119-127.	
Encouraging Songs	Glow and float, page 129	
Appreciating Songs	Any song, pages 139-147.	
Baby talk		

Weekly Journal

Dates: ________________

I Treasure God

I Treasure My Partner

"You formed my inmost being; you knit me in my mother's womb. I praise you, so wonderfully you have made me; wonderful are your works!" Psalm 139:13-14

Weekly Journal

Dates: ________________

I Treasure My Unborn Baby

____

____

____

____

____

____

____

____

____

I Treasure Me

____

____

____

____

____

____

____

____

____

Week 7

Your Baby Grows This Week

Then God whispers, "Let the baby's body continue to develop." And so it happens, your baby's ears and eyes become more defined. His eyelids and her tongue begin to form. An average baby is about one-third inch long. Sunday comes and Saturday follows, the seventh week.

What Your Partner Might Experience This Week

At seven weeks, expecting moms typically continue to experience morning sickness, frequent urination, and changes to her cervix. She may begin to exhibit a "pregnancy glow" as her face looks more rosy and shiny from increased blood flow.

Use the LOVE Compass to listen to your partner and observe her emotions and stress levels. Then, form your treasuring plan so she can feel your love and care for her and your baby.

"Love one another as I have loved you." John 13:34

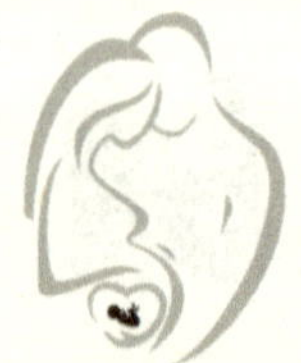

This Week's Treasuring Plan

Each day this week, St. Joseph help me to be:

Loving • Joyful • Peaceful • Patient • Kind • Generous • Faithful • Gentle • Self-Controlled

Strategy: Admire • Encourage • Appreciate

The Mary/St. Joseph songs I will listen to this week:	Any songs, pages 15-45

For My Life Partner

The Music I Am Making	What I Am Composing	Done
Daily Prayers	See pages 86-87.	
Finding Melody of Connection (Page 58)		
Writing Lyrics to Treasure (Page 59)		
Making Notation (Page 60)		
Rehearsing Your Love (Page 61)		
Performing in Person (Page 62)		

For My Unborn Baby

Affirming Action	What I Am Composing	Done
Daily Prayers	See pages 86-87.	
Words	See pages 111-114.	
Admiring Songs	Any song, pages 119-127.	
Encouraging Songs	Glow and float, page 129.	
Appreciating Songs	Any song, pages 139-147.	
Baby talk		

Weekly Journal

Dates: ________________

I Treasure God

I Treasure My Partner

Weekly Journal

Dates: ________________

I Treasure My Unborn Baby

I Treasure Me

Week 8

Your Baby Grows This Week

Then God whispers, "Let the baby's body take greater shape." And so it happens, your baby's body begins to straighten out and his/her face becomes more defined. Tiny buds of your baby's fingers and toes start to form. Her/his body is up to three-quarters of an inch long. Sunday comes and Saturday follows, the eighth week.

What Your Partner Might Experience This Week

At eight weeks, expecting moms typically continue to experience morning sickness, mood swings, fatigue, cramps, dizziness, and breast changes as the milk-making tissues in her breasts grow.

Use the LOVE Compass to listen to your partner and observe her emotions and stress levels. Then, form your treasuring plan so she can feel your love and care for her and your baby.

"Love one another as I have loved you." John 13:34

This Week's Treasuring Plan

Each day this week, St. Joseph help me to be:

Loving • Joyful • Peaceful • Patient • Kind
• Generous • Faithful • Gentle • Self-Controlled

Strategy: Admire • Encourage • Appreciate

The Mary/St. Joseph songs I will listen to this week:	Any songs, pages 15-45

For My Life Partner

The Music I Am Making	What I Am Composing	Done
Daily Prayers	See pages 86-87.	
Finding Melody of Connection (Page 74)		
Writing Lyrics to Treasure (Page 75)		
Making Notation (Page 76)		
Rehearsing Your Love (Page 77)		
Performing in Person (Page 78)		

For My Unborn Baby

Affirming Action	What I Am Composing	Done
Daily Prayers	See pages 86-87.	
Words	See pages 111-114.	
Admiring Songs	Any song, pages 119-127.	
Encouraging Songs	Two Months Now, page 133. My Precious One, Month 2, page 138.	
Appreciating Songs	Any song, pages 139-147.	
Baby talk		

Weekly Journal

Dates: ________________

I Treasure God

I Treasure My Partner

Weekly Journal

Dates: ________________

I Treasure My Unborn Baby

____

____

____

____

____

____

____

____

____

I Treasure Me

____

____

____

____

____

____

____

____

____

Week 9

Your Baby Grows This Week

Then God whispers, "Let the baby begin to move." And so it happens. His/her fingers and toes become more visible. Your baby begins to move, bend, and wiggle. Your baby's heart and arteries continue to develop. An average baby is about one inch long. Sunday comes and Saturday follows, the ninth week.

What Your Partner Might Experience This Week

At nine weeks, expecting moms typically continue to experience fatigue, frequent urination, mood swings, heartburn, and itchy breasts. Morning sickness tends to peak this week.

Use the LOVE Compass to listen to your partner and observe her emotions and stress levels. Then, form your treasuring plan so she can feel your love and care for her and your baby.

"Love one another as I have loved you." John 13:34

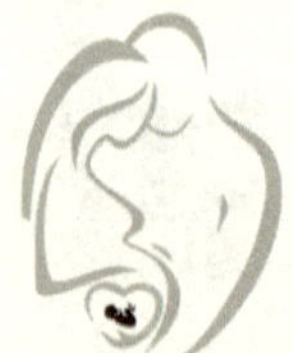

This Week's Treasuring Plan

Each day this week, St. Joseph help me to be:

Loving • Joyful • Peaceful • Patient • Kind
• Generous • Faithful • Gentle • Self-Controlled

Strategy: Admire • Encourage • Appreciate

The Mary/St. Joseph songs I will listen to this week:	Any songs, pages 15-45

For My Life Partner

The Music I Am Making	What I Am Composing	Done
Daily Prayers	See pages 86-87.	
Finding Melody of Connection (Page 74)		
Writing Lyrics to Treasure (Page 75)		
Making Notation (Page 76)		
Rehearsing Your Love (Page 77)		
Performing in Person (Page 78)		

For My Unborn Baby

Affirming Action	What I Am Composing	Done
Daily Prayers	See pages 86-87.	
Words	See pages 111-114.	
Admiring Songs	Any song, pages 119-127.	
Encouraging Songs	Two Months Now, page 133. My Precious One, Month 2, page 138.	
Appreciating Songs	Any song, pages 139-147.	
Baby talk		

Weekly Journal

Dates: ________________

I Treasure God

____

____

____

____

____

____

____

____

____

I Treasure My Partner

____

____

____

____

____

____

____

____

____

"You formed my inmost being; you knit me in my mother's womb. I praise you, so wonderfully you have made me; wonderful are your works!" Psalm 139:13-14

Weekly Journal

Dates: ________________

I Treasure My Unborn Baby

I Treasure Me

Week 10

Your Baby Grows This Week

Then God whispers, "Let the baby's body grow more defined." And so it happens, your baby's nose, eyes, and mouth take shape. His toes grow longer and her outer ears start to form. An average baby is about 1.5 inches long. Sunday comes and Saturday follows, the tenth week.

What Your Partner Might Experience This Week

At ten weeks, expecting moms typically continue to experience morning sickness, fatigue, increased urination, and constipation. She may begin to have weird dreams, headaches, and sleep issues as hormone changes occur in her body and the baby grows larger.

Use the LOVE Compass to listen to your partner and observe her emotions and stress levels. Then, form your treasuring plan so she can feel your love and care for her and your baby.

"Love one another as I have loved you." John 13:34

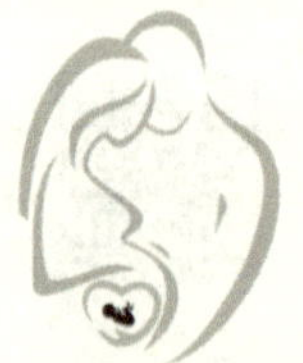

This Week's Treasuring Plan

Each day this week, St. Joseph help me to be:

Loving • Joyful • Peaceful • Patient • Kind • Generous • Faithful • Gentle • Self-Controlled

Strategy: Admire • Encourage • Appreciate

The Mary/St. Joseph songs I will listen to this week:	Any songs, pages 15-45

For My Life Partner

The Music I Am Making	What I Am Composing	Done
Daily Prayers	See pages 86-87.	
Finding Melody of Connection (Page 74)		
Writing Lyrics to Treasure (Page 75)		
Making Notation (Page 76)		
Rehearsing Your Love (Page 77)		
Performing in Person (Page 78)		

For My Unborn Baby

Affirming Action	What I Am Composing	Done
Daily Prayers	See pages 86-87.	
Words	See pages 111-114.	
Admiring Songs	Any song, pages 119-127.	
Encouraging Songs	Two Months Now, page 138. My Precious One, Month 2, page 133.	
Appreciating Songs	Any song, pages 139-147.	
Baby talk		

Weekly Journal

Dates: ________________

I Treasure God

I Treasure My Partner

"You formed my inmost being; you knit me in my mother's womb. I praise you, so wonderfully you have made me; wonderful are your works!" Psalm 139:13-14

Weekly Journal

Dates: ________________

I Treasure My Unborn Baby

____

____

____

____

____

____

____

____

____

I Treasure Me

____

____

____

____

____

____

____

____

____

Week 11

Your Baby Grows This Week

Then God whispers, "Let the baby's physical senses grow." And so it happens, your baby's taste buds begin to develop and her/his eyelids close. An average baby's body is about two inches long. Sunday comes and Saturday follows, the eleventh week.

What Your Partner Might Experience This Week

At eleven weeks, expecting moms typically experience lingering nausea and mood swings. Her belly may begin to show her "baby bump." Your partner's hair may grow faster and thicker; her nails may grow longer and stronger.

Use the LOVE Compass to listen to your partner and observe her emotions and stress levels. Then, form your treasuring plan so she can feel your love and care for her and your baby.

"Love one another as I have loved you." John 13:34

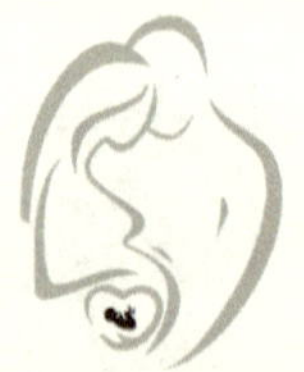

This Week's Treasuring Plan

Each day this week, St. Joseph help me to be:

Loving • Joyful • Peaceful • Patient • Kind • Generous • Faithful • Gentle • Self-Controlled

Strategy: Admire • Encourage • Appreciate

The Mary/St. Joseph songs I will listen to this week:	Any songs, pages 15-45

For My Life Partner

The Music I Am Making	What I Am Composing	Done
Daily Prayers	See pages 86-87.	
Finding Melody of Connection (Page 74)		
Writing Lyrics to Treasure (Page 75)		
Making Notation (Page 76)		
Rehearsing Your Love (Page 77)		
Performing in Person (Page 78)		

For My Unborn Baby

Affirming Action	What I Am Composing	Done
Daily Prayers	See pages 86-87.	
Words	See pages 111-114.	
Admiring Songs	Any song, pages 119-127.	
Encouraging Songs	Two Months Now, page 138. My Precious One, Month 2, page 133.	
Appreciating Songs	Any song, pages 139-147.	
Baby talk		

Weekly Journal

Dates: ________________

I Treasure God

I Treasure My Partner

"You formed my inmost being; you knit me in my mother's womb. I praise you, so wonderfully you have made me; wonderful are your works!" Psalm 139:13-14

Weekly Journal

Dates: ________________

I Treasure My Unborn Baby

____

____

____

____

____

____

____

____

____

I Treasure Me

____

____

____

____

____

____

____

____

____

Week 12

Your Baby Grows This Week

Then God whispers, "Let the structure of the baby's body grow stronger." And so it happens, your baby's bones become harder. Her/his vocal cords and fingernails start to form. An average baby's body is about two inches and a half long. Sunday comes and Saturday follows, the twelfth week.

What Your Partner Might Experience This Week

At twelve weeks, expecting moms typically experience less nausea, although your partner may continue to experience it. Her uterus is expanding and she may feel relief in her bladder. She may develop changes in skin color with dark patches on her face.

Use the LOVE Compass to listen to your partner and observe her emotions and stress levels. Then, form your treasuring plan so she can feel your love and care for her and your baby.

"Love one another as I have loved you." John 13:34

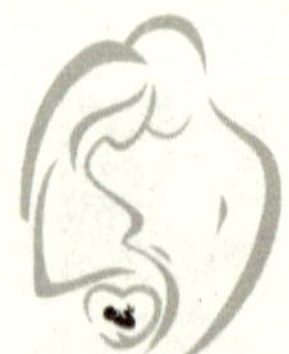

This Week's Treasuring Plan

Each day this week, St. Joseph help me to be:

Loving • Joyful • Peaceful • Patient • Kind • Generous • Faithful • Gentle • Self-Controlled

Strategy: Admire • Encourage • Appreciate

The Mary/St. Joseph songs I will listen to this week:	Any songs, pages 15-45

For My Life Partner

The Music I Am Making	What I Am Composing	Done
Daily Prayers	See pages 86-87.	
Finding Melody of Connection (Page 74)		
Writing Lyrics to Treasure (Page 75)		
Making Notation (Page 76)		
Rehearsing Your Love (Page 77)		
Performing in Person (Page 78)		

For My Unborn Baby

Affirming Action	What I Am Composing	Done
Daily Prayers	See pages 86-87.	
Words	See pages 111-114.	
Admiring Songs	Any song, pages 119-127.	
Encouraging Songs	Three Months Now, page 138. My Precious One, Month 3, page 133.	
Appreciating Songs	Any song, pages 139-147.	
Baby talk		

Weekly Journal

Dates: ________________

I Treasure God

I Treasure My Partner

"You formed my inmost being; you knit me in my mother's womb. I praise you, so wonderfully you have made me; wonderful are your works!" Psalm 139:13-14

Weekly Journal

Dates: ________________

I Treasure My Unborn Baby

I Treasure Me

Week 13

Your Baby Grows This Week

Then God whispers, "Let the baby start to swallow." And so it happens, your baby begins to swallow so that she/he can eat after birth. Your baby's fingertips begin to develop ridges that will become unique fingerprints. An average baby's body is about three inches long. Sunday comes and Saturday follows, the thirteenth week.

What Your Partner Might Experience This Week

At thirteen weeks, expecting moms typically continue to experience constipation or heartburn, vaginal discharges, and stretch marks.

Use the LOVE Compass to listen to your partner and observe her emotions and stress levels. Then, form your treasuring plan so she can feel your love and care for her and your baby.

"Love one another as I have loved you." John 13:34

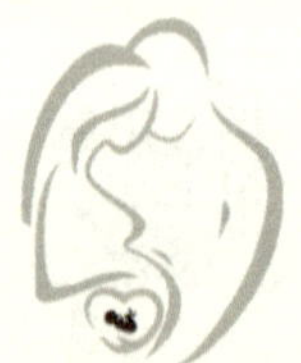

This Week's Treasuring Plan

Each day this week, St. Joseph help me to be:

Loving • Joyful • Peaceful • Patient • Kind • Generous • Faithful • Gentle • Self-Controlled

Strategy: Admire • Encourage • Appreciate

The Mary/St. Joseph songs I will listen to this week:	Any songs, pages 15-45

For My Life Partner

The Music I Am Making	What I Am Composing	Done
Daily Prayers	See pages 86-87.	
Finding Melody of Connection (Page 74)		
Writing Lyrics to Treasure (Page 75)		
Making Notation (Page 76)		
Rehearsing Your Love (Page 77)		
Performing in Person (Page 78)		

For My Unborn Baby

Affirming Action	What I Am Composing	Done
Daily Prayers	See pages 86-87.	
Words	See pages 111-114.	
Admiring Songs	Any song, pages 119-127.	
Encouraging Songs	Three Months Now, page 138. My Precious One, Month 3, page 133.	
Appreciating Songs	Any song, pages 139-147.	
Baby talk		

Weekly Journal

Dates: ________________

I Treasure God

I Treasure My Partner

"You formed my inmost being; you knit me in my mother's womb. I praise you, so wonderfully you have made me; wonderful are your works!" Psalm 139:13-14

Weekly Journal

Dates: ________________

I Treasure My Unborn Baby

____

____

____

____

____

____

____

____

____

I Treasure Me

____

____

____

____

____

____

____

____

____

Week 14

Your Baby Grows This Week

Then God whispers, "Let the baby begin to express itself." And so it happens. Your baby begins to move his/her body more. She wiggles and he stretches. Your baby begins to frown, squint, and pucker. Her/his thyroid gland begins to make hormones. An average baby is three-and-a-half inches long and weighs about three ounces. Sunday comes and Saturday follows, the fourteenth week.

What Your Partner Might Experience This Week

At fourteen weeks, expecting moms typically experience more energy as nausea and fatigue lessen. Her breast tenderness starts to ease. Her sexual desire may return. New skin moles may develop or existing ones may get larger or darker.

Use the LOVE Compass to listen to your partner and observe her emotions and stress levels. Then, form your treasuring plan so she can feel your love and care for her and your baby.

"Love one another as I have loved you." John 13:34

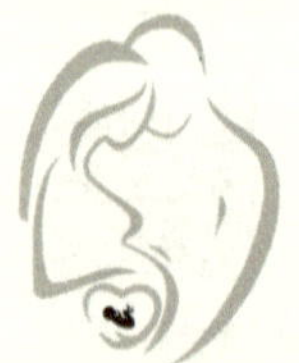

This Week's Treasuring Plan

Each day this week, St. Joseph help me to be:

Loving • Joyful • Peaceful • Patient • Kind
• Generous • Faithful • Gentle • Self-Controlled

Strategy: Admire • Encourage • Appreciate

The Mary/St. Joseph songs I will listen to this week:	Any songs, pages 15-45

For My Life Partner

The Music I Am Making	What I Am Composing	Done
Daily Prayers	See pages 86-87.	
Finding Melody of Connection (Page 74)		
Writing Lyrics to Treasure (Page 75)		
Making Notation (Page 76)		
Rehearsing Your Love (Page 77)		
Performing in Person (Page 78)		

For My Unborn Baby

Affirming Action	What I Am Composing	Done
Daily Prayers	See pages 86-87.	
Words	See pages 111-114.	
Admiring Songs	Any song, pages 119-127.	
Encouraging Songs	Three Months Now, page 138. My Precious One, Month 3, page 133.	
Appreciating Songs	Any song, pages 139-147.	
Baby talk		

Weekly Journal

Dates: ________________

I Treasure God

____

____

____

____

____

____

____

____

____

I Treasure My Partner

____

____

____

____

____

____

____

____

____

Weekly Journal

Dates: ________________

I Treasure My Unborn Baby

I Treasure Me

Week 15

Your Baby Grows This Week

Then God whispers, "Let the baby enjoy its body." And so it happens, your baby begins to move his/her entire body. His arms. Her legs. Your baby could stretch. His/her ears become more distinct. An average baby is nearly 6.5 inches long (from crown to heel) and weighs nearly 4 ounces. Sunday comes and Saturday follows, the fifteenth week.

What Your Partner Might Experience This Week

At fifteen weeks, expecting moms typically experience noticeable weight gain, bleeding gums or nosebleeds. Many pregnant women continue to feel dizziness, headaches and heartburn.

Use the LOVE Compass to listen to your partner and observe her emotions and stress levels. Then, form your treasuring plan so she can feel your love and care for her and your baby.

"Love one another as I have loved you." John 13:34

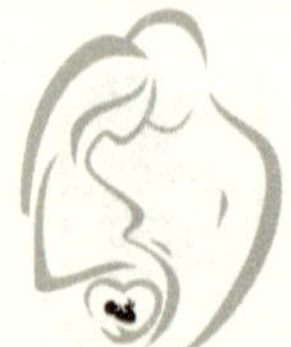

This Week's Treasuring Plan

Each day this week, St. Joseph help me to be:

Loving • Joyful • Peaceful • Patient • Kind • Generous • Faithful • Gentle • Self-Controlled

Strategy: Admire • Encourage • Appreciate

The Mary/St. Joseph songs I will listen to this week:	Any songs, pages 15-45

For My Life Partner

The Music I Am Making	What I Am Composing	Done
Daily Prayers	See pages 86-87.	
Finding Melody of Connection (Page 74)		
Writing Lyrics to Treasure (Page 75)		
Making Notation (Page 76)		
Rehearsing Your Love (Page 77)		
Performing in Person (Page 78)		

For My Unborn Baby

Affirming Action	What I Am Composing	Done
Daily Prayers	See pages 86-87.	
Words	See pages 111-114.	
Admiring Songs	Any song, pages 119-127.	
Encouraging Songs	Three Months Now, page 138. My Precious One, Month 3, page 133.	
Appreciating Songs	Any song, pages 139-147.	
Baby talk		

Weekly Journal

Dates: ________________

I Treasure God

I Treasure My Partner

"You formed my inmost being; you knit me in my mother's womb. I praise you, so wonderfully you have made me; wonderful are your works!" Psalm 139:13-14

Weekly Journal

Dates: ________________

I Treasure My Unborn Baby

I Treasure Me

Week 16

Your Baby Grows This Week

Then God whispers, "Let the baby begin to taste and hear." And so it happens, your baby starts to taste the amniotic fluid and what Mom ate. He begins to hear sounds faintly. Her eyebrows grow hair. An average baby is about seven inches long and weighs about 5 ounces. Sunday comes and Saturday follows, the sixteenth week.

What Your Partner Might Experience This Week

At sixteen weeks, expecting moms typically continue to experience previous week's symptoms of nosebleeds, bleeding gums, dizziness, gas, headaches and heartburn. She may begin to feel baby flutters as your baby is moving quite a bit. Her baby bump is getting larger. She may begin to have food cravings, now that the nausea has subsided.

Use the LOVE Compass to listen to your partner and observe her emotions and stress levels. Then, form your treasuring plan so she can feel your love and care for her and your baby.

"Love one another as I have loved you." John 13:34

This Week's Treasuring Plan

Each day this week, St. Joseph help me to be:

Loving • Joyful • Peaceful • Patient • Kind • Generous • Faithful • Gentle • Self-Controlled

Strategy: Admire • Encourage • Appreciate

The Mary/St. Joseph songs I will listen to this week:	Any songs, pages 15-45

For My Life Partner

The Music I Am Making	What I Am Composing	Done
Daily Prayers	See pages 86-87.	
Finding Melody of Connection (Page 74)		
Writing Lyrics to Treasure (Page 75)		
Making Notation (Page 76)		
Rehearsing Your Love (Page 77)		
Performing in Person (Page 78)		

For My Unborn Baby

Affirming Action	What I Am Composing	Done
Daily Prayers	See pages 86-87.	
Words	See pages 111-114.	
Admiring Songs	Any song, pages 119-127.	
Encouraging Songs	Taste and Ears are Working Now, page 130.	
Appreciating Songs	Any song, pages 139-147.	
Baby talk		

"You are precious in my eyes and I love you." Isaiah 43:4

Weekly Journal

Dates: ________________

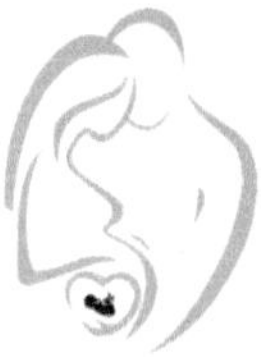

I Treasure God

____

____

____

____

____

____

____

____

____

I Treasure My Partner

____

____

____

____

____

____

____

____

____

"You formed my inmost being; you knit me in my mother's womb. I praise you, so wonderfully you have made me; wonderful are your works!" Psalm 139:13-14

Weekly Journal

Dates: ________________

I Treasure My Unborn Baby

I Treasure Me

Week 17

Your Baby Grows This Week

Then God whispers, "Let the baby's body start to protect itself." And so it happens. Your baby's body begins to make fat cells to store energy and keep warm. She/he begins to use her/his mouth to make sucking movements to feed after being born. An average baby's body is about 7.75 inches long and weighs over 6 ounces. Sunday comes and Saturday follows, the seventeenth week.

What Your Partner Might Experience This Week

At seventeen weeks, expecting moms may continue to experience the discomforts of heartburn, bleeding gums, nosebleeds or headaches or they may have none of those symptoms. Your partner may feel nasal congestion, as well as pain in her lower back and pelvis area.

Use the LOVE Compass to listen to your partner and observe her emotions and stress levels. Then, form your treasuring plan so she can feel your love and care for her and your baby.

"Love one another as I have loved you." John 13:34

This Week's Treasuring Plan

Each day this week, St. Joseph help me to be:

Loving • Joyful • Peaceful • Patient • Kind • Generous • Faithful • Gentle • Self-Controlled

Strategy: Admire • Encourage • Appreciate

The Mary/St. Joseph songs I will listen to this week:	Any songs, pages 15-45

For My Life Partner

The Music I Am Making	What I Am Composing	Done
Daily Prayers	See pages 86-87.	
Finding Melody of Connection (Page 74)		
Writing Lyrics to Treasure (Page 75)		
Making Notation (Page 76)		
Rehearsing Your Love (Page 77)		
Performing in Person (Page 78)		

For My Unborn Baby

Affirming Action	What I Am Composing	Done
Daily Prayers	See pages 86-87.	
Words	See pages 111-114.	
Admiring Songs	Any song, pages 119-127.	
Encouraging Songs	Four Months Now, page 138. My Precious One, Month 4, page 133.	
Appreciating Songs	Any song, pages 139-147.	
Baby talk		

Weekly Journal

Dates: ________________

I Treasure God

I Treasure My Partner

Weekly Journal

Dates: ________________

I Treasure My Unborn Baby

I Treasure Me

Week 18

Your Baby Grows This Week

Then God whispers, "Let the baby learn to rest." And so it happens. Your baby begins practicing how to nap. Her/his nerves put on a coat of myelin. The doctor can accurately determine your baby's gender. An a baby's average body is 8.33 inches long and weighs nearly 8 ounces. Sunday comes and Saturday follows, the eighteenth week.

What Your Partner Might Experience This Week

At eighteen weeks, expecting moms typically experience some off-balance, feeling faint and dizzy as their bodies change. She may feel a dip in her blood pressure, as well as increased movement of your baby. Her baby bump is expanding.

Use the LOVE Compass to listen to your partner and observe her emotions and stress levels. Then, form your treasuring plan so she can feel your love and care for her and your baby.

"Love one another as I have loved you." John 13:34

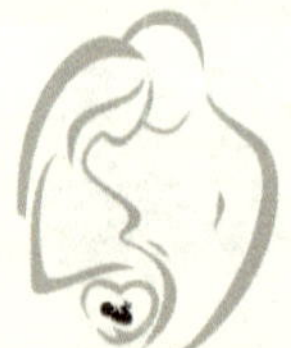

This Week's Treasuring Plan

Each day this week, St. Joseph help me to be:

Loving • Joyful • Peaceful • Patient • Kind • Generous • Faithful • Gentle • Self-Controlled

Strategy: Admire • Encourage • Appreciate

The Mary/St. Joseph songs I will listen to this week:	Any songs, pages 15-45

For My Life Partner

The Music I Am Making	What I Am Composing	Done
Daily Prayers	See pages 86-87.	
Finding Melody of Connection (Page 74)		
Writing Lyrics to Treasure (Page 75)		
Making Notation (Page 76)		
Rehearsing Your Love (Page 77)		
Performing in Person (Page 78)		

For My Unborn Baby

Affirming Action	What I Am Composing	Done
Daily Prayers	See pages 86-87.	
Words	See pages 111-114.	
Admiring Songs	Any song, pages 119-127.	
Encouraging Songs	My Baby Rests and Naps, page 132. My Precious One, Month 4, page 133.	
Appreciating Songs	Any song, pages 139-147.	
Baby talk		

Weekly Journal

Dates: ________________

I Treasure God

I Treasure My Partner

"You formed my inmost being; you knit me in my mother's womb. I praise you, so wonderfully you have made me; wonderful are your works!" Psalm 139:13-14

Weekly Journal

Dates: ________________

I Treasure My Unborn Baby

____

____

____

____

____

____

____

____

____

I Treasure Me

____

____

____

____

____

____

____

____

____

Week 19

Your Baby Grows This Week

Then God whispers, "Let the baby grow hair and teeth." And so it happens. The hair on your baby's head starts to be visible so that God can count every one of them. Her/his tiny teeth develop below her/his gums. Your baby's body makes brown fat to keep warm after birth. An average baby is nine inches long and weighs nearly 9.5 ounces. Sunday comes and Saturday follows, the nineteenth week

What Your Partner Might Experience This Week

At nineteen weeks, expecting moms typically experience heartburn, bleeding gums, nasal congestion, and food cravings. Pregnant women feel ligament pain in their lower belly or groin area, and stretching of the uterus. Your partner may feel forgetful, confused, have difficulty focusing with "foggy brain."

Use the LOVE Compass to listen to your partner and observe her emotions and stress levels. Then, form your treasuring plan so she can feel your love and care for her and your baby.

"Love one another as I have loved you." John 13:34

This Week's Treasuring Plan

Each day this week, St. Joseph help me to be:

Loving • Joyful • Peaceful • Patient • Kind • Generous • Faithful • Gentle • Self-Controlled

Strategy: Admire • Encourage • Appreciate

The Mary/St. Joseph songs I will listen to this week:	Any songs, pages 15-45

For My Life Partner

The Music I Am Making	What I Am Composing	Done
Daily Prayers	See pages 86-87.	
Finding Melody of Connection (Page 74)		
Writing Lyrics to Treasure (Page 75)		
Making Notation (Page 76)		
Rehearsing Your Love (Page 77)		
Performing in Person (Page 78)		

For My Unborn Baby

Affirming Action	What I Am Composing	Done
Daily Prayers	See pages 86-87.	
Words	See pages 111-114.	
Admiring Songs	Any song, pages 119-127.	
Encouraging Songs	Hair and Teeth Are Growing Now, page 130.	
Appreciating Songs	Any song, pages 139-147.	
Baby talk		

Weekly Journal

Dates: ________________

I Treasure God

I Treasure My Partner

Weekly Journal

Dates: ________________

I Treasure My Unborn Baby

I Treasure Me

Week 20

Your Baby Grows This Week

Then God whispers, "Let the baby's internal organs continue to develop." And so it happens. Your baby's reproductive system develops. His sweat glands form, and her gallbladder produces bile to digest nutrients. An average baby's body is 9.5 inches long and weighs nearly 11.5 ounces. Sunday comes and Saturday follows, the twentieth week.

What Your Partner Might Experience This Week

At twenty weeks, expecting moms may continue to experience heartburn, bleeding gums, "foggy brain," nasal congestion, and food cravings. Pregnant women may feel leg cramps and greater weight gain. Her belly button shape may change. After week 13, expecting moms may gain one pound a week for the rest of their pregnancy.

Use the LOVE Compass to listen to your partner and observe her emotions and stress levels. Then, form your treasuring plan so she can feel your love and care for her and your baby.

"Love one another as I have loved you." John 13:34

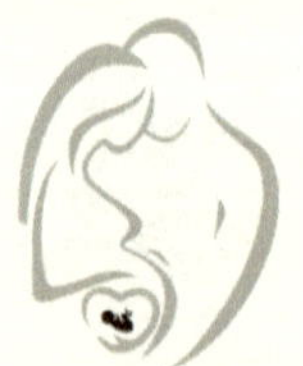

This Week's Treasuring Plan

Each day this week, St. Joseph help me to be:

Loving • Joyful • Peaceful • Patient • Kind • Generous • Faithful • Gentle • Self-Controlled

Strategy: Admire • Encourage • Appreciate

The Mary/St. Joseph songs I will listen to this week:	Any songs, pages 15-45

For My Life Partner

The Music I Am Making	What I Am Composing	Done
Daily Prayers	See pages 86-87.	
Finding Melody of Connection (Page 74)		
Writing Lyrics to Treasure (Page 75)		
Making Notation (Page 76)		
Rehearsing Your Love (Page 77)		
Performing in Person (Page 78)		

For My Unborn Baby

Affirming Action	What I Am Composing	Done
Daily Prayers	See pages 86-87.	
Words	See pages 111-114.	
Admiring Songs	Any song, pages 119-127.	
Encouraging Songs	Five Months Now, page 138. My Precious One, Month 5, page 133.	
Appreciating Songs	Any song, pages 139-147.	
Baby talk		

Weekly Journal

Dates: _______________

I Treasure God

____

____

____

____

____

____

____

____

____

I Treasure My Partner

____

____

____

____

____

____

____

____

____

"You formed my inmost being; you knit me in my mother's womb. I praise you, so wonderfully you have made me; wonderful are your works!" Psalm 139:13-14

Weekly Journal

Dates: ____________________

I Treasure My Unborn Baby

____

____

____

____

____

____

____

____

____

I Treasure Me

____

____

____

____

____

____

____

____

____

Week 21

Your Baby Grows This Week

Then God whispers, "Let the baby learn to digest." And so it happens. Your baby's pancreas begins to make digestive enzymes and his/her small intestine absorbs nutrients from the amniotic fluid. An average baby's body is 10 inches long and weighs nearly 14 ounces. Sunday comes and Saturday follows, the twenty-first week.

What Your Partner Might Experience This Week

At twenty-one weeks, expecting moms may continue to experience heartburn, bleeding gums, "foggy brain," nasal congestion, leg cramps, backaches, and food cravings. Your partner may feel swelling in her legs, feet, or ankles. She may note varicose veins in her legs, vulva, or rectum.

Use the LOVE Compass to listen to your partner and observe her emotions and stress levels. Then, form your treasuring plan so she can feel your love and care for her and your baby.

"Love one another as I have loved you." John 13:34

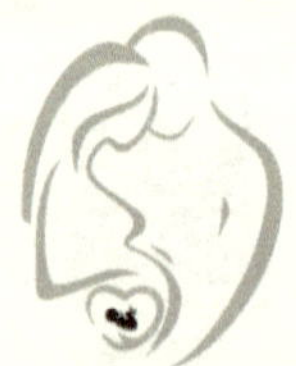

This Week's Treasuring Plan

Each day this week, St. Joseph help me to be:

Loving • Joyful • Peaceful • Patient • Kind • Generous • Faithful • Gentle • Self-Controlled

Strategy: Admire • Encourage • Appreciate

The Mary/St. Joseph songs I will listen to this week:	Any songs, pages 15-45

For My Life Partner

The Music I Am Making	What I Am Composing	Done
Daily Prayers	See pages 86-87.	
Finding Melody of Connection (Page 74)		
Writing Lyrics to Treasure (Page 75)		
Making Notation (Page 76)		
Rehearsing Your Love (Page 77)		
Performing in Person (Page 78)		

For My Unborn Baby

Affirming Action	What I Am Composing	Done
Daily Prayers	See pages 86-87.	
Words	See pages 111-114.	
Admiring Songs	Any song, pages 119-127.	
Encouraging Songs	Precious Baby, Learn to Eat, page 135.	
Appreciating Songs	Any song, pages 139-147.	
Baby talk		

Weekly Journal

Dates: ________________

I Treasure God

I Treasure My Partner

"You formed my inmost being; you knit me in my mother's womb. I praise you, so wonderfully you have made me; wonderful are your works!" Psalm 139:13-14

Weekly Journal

Dates: ________________

I Treasure My Unborn Baby

____

____

____

____

____

____

____

____

____

I Treasure Me

____

____

____

____

____

____

____

____

____

Week 22

Your Baby Grows This Week

Then God whispers, "Let the baby become more expressive." And so it happens. Your baby moves her/his hands freely, touching and crossing each other, even grasping the umbilical cord. Your baby's tear ducts grow. The doctor can hear her/his heartbeat through a stethoscope. An average baby's body is 10.75 inches long and weighs around 16 ounces. Sunday comes and Saturday follows, the twenty-second week.

What Your Partner Might Experience This Week

At twenty-two weeks, expecting moms may continue to experience heartburn, bleeding gums, "foggy brain," nasal congestion, leg cramps, backaches, and food cravings. Your partner may begin to feel normal Braxton Hicks contractions in her uterus, which are strong and irregular.

Use the LOVE Compass to listen to your partner and observe her emotions and stress levels. Then, form your treasuring plan so she can feel your love and care for her and your baby.

"Love one another as I have loved you." John 13:34

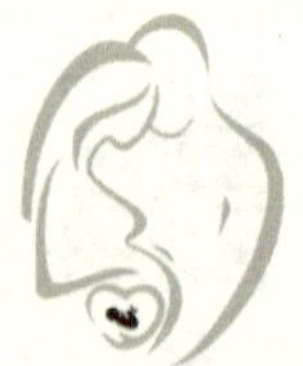

This Week's Treasuring Plan

Each day this week, St. Joseph help me to be:

Loving • Joyful • Peaceful • Patient • Kind
• Generous • Faithful • Gentle • Self-Controlled

Strategy: Admire • Encourage • Appreciate

The Mary/St. Joseph songs I will listen to this week:	Any songs, pages 15-45

For My Life Partner

The Music I Am Making	What I Am Composing	Done
Daily Prayers	See pages 86-87.	
Finding Melody of Connection (Page 74)		
Writing Lyrics to Treasure (Page 75)		
Making Notation (Page 76)		
Rehearsing Your Love (Page 77)		
Performing in Person (Page 78)		

For My Unborn Baby

Affirming Action	What I Am Composing	Done
Daily Prayers	See pages 86-87.	
Words	See pages 111-114.	
Admiring Songs	Any song, pages 119-127.	
Encouraging Songs	Precious Baby, Move Your Hands, page 136.	
Appreciating Songs	Any song, pages 139-147.	
Baby talk		

Weekly Journal

Dates: ________________

I Treasure God

I Treasure My Partner

"You formed my inmost being; you knit me in my mother's womb. I praise you, so wonderfully you have made me; wonderful are your works!" Psalm 139:13-14

Weekly Journal

Dates: ________________

I Treasure My Unborn Baby

I Treasure Me

Week 23

Your Baby Grows This Week

Then God whispers, "Let the baby become stronger in mind and body." And so it happens. Your baby's muscles, brain, and fingernails grow rapidly and his/her eyes respond to light outside Mom's womb. An average baby's body is over 11 inches long and weighs around 20 ounces. Sunday comes and Saturday follows, the twenty-third week.

What Your Partner Might Experience This Week

At twenty-three weeks, expecting moms may continue to experience symptoms like leg cramps, forgetfulness, and food cravings. Your partner may feel start to feel hot flashes. Her eyesight may be blurry or she may feel dry or irritation in her eyes.

Use the LOVE Compass to listen to your partner and observe her emotions and stress levels. Then, form your treasuring plan so she can feel your love and care for her and your baby.

"Love one another as I have loved you." John 13:34

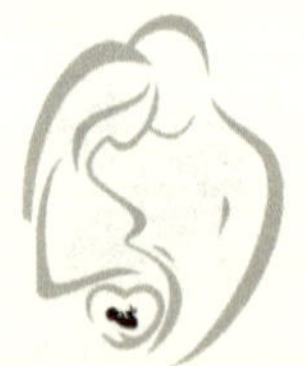

This Week's Treasuring Plan

Each day this week, St. Joseph help me to be:

Loving • Joyful • Peaceful • Patient • Kind
• Generous • Faithful • Gentle • Self-Controlled

Strategy: Admire • Encourage • Appreciate

The Mary/St. Joseph songs I will listen to this week:	Any songs, pages 15-45

For My Life Partner

The Music I Am Making	What I Am Composing	Done
Daily Prayers	See pages 86-87.	
Finding Melody of Connection (Page 74)		
Writing Lyrics to Treasure (Page 75)		
Making Notation (Page 76)		
Rehearsing Your Love (Page 77)		
Performing in Person (Page 78)		

For My Unborn Baby

Affirming Action	What I Am Composing	Done
Daily Prayers	See pages 86-87.	
Words	See pages 111-114.	
Admiring Songs	Any song, pages 119-127.	
Encouraging Songs	Five Months Now, page 138. My Precious One, Month 5, page 133.	
Appreciating Songs	Any song, pages 139-147.	
Baby talk		

Weekly Journal

Dates: ________________

I Treasure God

I Treasure My Partner

"You formed my inmost being; you knit me in my mother's womb. I praise you, so wonderfully you have made me; wonderful are your works!" Psalm 139:13-14

Weekly Journal

Dates: ________________

I Treasure My Unborn Baby

I Treasure Me

Week 24

Your Baby Grows This Week

Then God whispers, "Let the baby get ready to breathe." And so it happens. Your baby's lungs form branches to inhale and exhale; your baby's ears and eyelids begin to take their final shape. An average baby's body is 12 inches long and weighs around 24 ounces. Sunday comes and Saturday follows, the twenty-fourth week.

What Your Partner Might Experience This Week

At twenty-four weeks, expecting moms may continue to experience symptoms like aches and pains, leg cramps, forgetfulness, Braxton Hicks contractions, and food cravings. Your partner may feel heartburn, reflux, or indigestion, along with linea negra, a black line over her tummy.

Use the LOVE Compass to listen to your partner and observe her emotions and stress levels. Then, form your treasuring plan so she can feel your love and care for her and your baby.

"Love one another as I have loved you." John 13:34

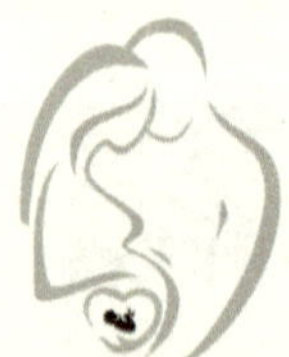

This Week's Treasuring Plan

Each day this week, St. Joseph help me to be:

Loving • Joyful • Peaceful • Patient • Kind • Generous • Faithful • Gentle • Self-Controlled

Strategy: Admire • Encourage • Appreciate

The Mary/St. Joseph songs I will listen to this week:	Any songs, pages 15-45

For My Life Partner

The Music I Am Making	What I Am Composing	Done
Daily Prayers	See pages 86-87.	
Finding Melody of Connection (Page 74)		
Writing Lyrics to Treasure (Page 75)		
Making Notation (Page 76)		
Rehearsing Your Love (Page 77)		
Performing in Person (Page 78)		

For My Unborn Baby

Affirming Action	What I Am Composing	Done
Daily Prayers	See pages 86-87.	
Words	See pages 111-114.	
Admiring Songs	Any song, pages 119-127.	
Encouraging Songs	My Baby's Lungs, page 132. Six Months Now, page 138.	
Appreciating Songs	Any song, pages 139-147.	
Baby talk		

Weekly Journal

Dates: ________________

I Treasure God

I Treasure My Partner

"You formed my inmost being; you knit me in my mother's womb. I praise you, so wonderfully you have made me; wonderful are your works!" Psalm 139:13-14

Weekly Journal

Dates: ____________________

I Treasure My Unborn Baby

____

____

____

____

____

____

____

____

____

I Treasure Me

____

____

____

____

____

____

____

____

____

Week 25

Your Baby Grows This Week

Then God whispers, "Let the baby learn to use the gift of smell." And so it happens. Your baby begins to notice and smell scents and odors in the amniotic fluid. His/her lungs grow more defined. An average baby's body is 12.5 inches long and weighs around 27 ounces. Sunday comes and Saturday follows, the twenty-fifth week.

What Your Partner Might Experience This Week

At twenty-five weeks, expecting moms may continue to experience symptoms like heartburn, leg cramps, forgetfulness, Braxton Hicks contractions, and vision changes. Your partner may feel the baby kicking more often. She may have heart palpitations, or fluttering. Her belly and breasts may feel itchy.

Use the LOVE Compass to listen to your partner and observe her emotions and stress levels. Then, form your treasuring plan so she can feel your love and care for her and your baby.

"Love one another as I have loved you." John 13:34

This Week's Treasuring Plan

Each day this week, St. Joseph help me to be:

Loving • Joyful • Peaceful • Patient • Kind
• Generous • Faithful • Gentle • Self-Controlled

Strategy: Admire • Encourage • Appreciate

The Mary/St. Joseph songs I will listen to this week:	Any songs, pages 15-45

For My Life Partner

The Music I Am Making	What I Am Composing	Done
Daily Prayers	See pages 86-87.	
Finding Melody of Connection (Page 74)		
Writing Lyrics to Treasure (Page 75)		
Making Notation (Page 76)		
Rehearsing Your Love (Page 77)		
Performing in Person (Page 78)		

For My Unborn Baby

Affirming Action	What I Am Composing	Done
Daily Prayers	See pages 86-87.	
Words	See pages 111-114.	
Admiring Songs	Any song, pages 119-127.	
Encouraging Songs	My Baby's Nose, page 132. Six Months Now, page 138.	
Appreciating Songs	Any song, pages 139-147.	
Baby talk		

Weekly Journal

Dates: ________________

I Treasure God

____

____

____

____

____

____

____

____

____

I Treasure My Partner

____

____

____

____

____

____

____

____

____

"You formed my inmost being; you knit me in my mother's womb. I praise you, so wonderfully you have made me; wonderful are your works!" Psalm 139:13-14

Weekly Journal

Dates: ________________

I Treasure My Unborn Baby

I Treasure Me

Week 26

Your Baby Grows This Week

Then God whispers, "Let the baby's eyes mature and let her use the gift of reflex." And so it happens. Your baby's eyes become fully developed with eyebrows and eyelashes. She/he begins to use the startle reflex to react to loud sounds. An average baby's body is about 13 inches long and weighs around 32 ounces. Sunday comes and Saturday follows, the twenty-sixth week.

What Your Partner Might Experience This Week

At twenty-six weeks, expecting moms may continue to experience symptoms like heartburn, leg cramps, forgetfulness, Braxton Hicks contractions, and vision changes. Your partner may feel more pain in her ribs. She may have more stretch marks which may feel itchy or burning.

Use the LOVE Compass to listen to your partner and observe her emotions and stress levels. Then, form your treasuring plan so she can feel your love and care for her and your baby.

"Love one another as I have loved you." John 13:34

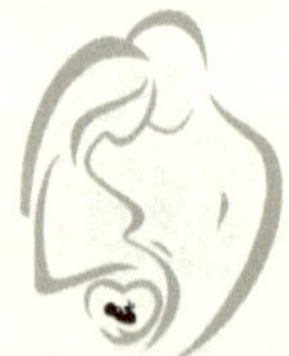

This Week's Treasuring Plan

Each day this week, St. Joseph help me to be:

Loving • Joyful • Peaceful • Patient • Kind
• Generous • Faithful • Gentle • Self-Controlled

Strategy: Admire • Encourage • Appreciate

The Mary/St. Joseph songs I will listen to this week:	Any songs, pages 15-45

For My Life Partner

The Music I Am Making	What I Am Composing	Done
Daily Prayers	See pages 86-87.	
Finding Melody of Connection (Page 74)		
Writing Lyrics to Treasure (Page 75)		
Making Notation (Page 76)		
Rehearsing Your Love (Page 77)		
Performing in Person (Page 78)		

For My Unborn Baby

Affirming Action	What I Am Composing	Done
Daily Prayers	See pages 86-87.	
Words	See pages 111-114.	
Admiring Songs	Any song, pages 119-127.	
Encouraging Songs	My Precious One, Month 6, page 134. Six Months Now, page 138.	
Appreciating Songs	Any song, pages 139-147.	
Baby talk		

Weekly Journal

Dates: ________________

I Treasure God

____

____

____

____

____

____

____

____

____

I Treasure My Partner

____

____

____

____

____

____

____

____

____

"You formed my inmost being; you knit me in my mother's womb. I praise you, so wonderfully you have made me; wonderful are your works!" Psalm 139:13-14

Weekly Journal

Dates: ________________

I Treasure My Unborn Baby

____

____

____

____

____

____

____

____

____

I Treasure Me

____

____

____

____

____

____

____

____

____

Week 27

Your Baby Grows This Week

Then God whispers, "Let the baby's brain form and let her use the gift of lungs to take breaths." And so it happens. Your baby's brain begins to form neurons and synapses. She/he starts practicing taking breaths of amniotic fluid to develop his/her lungs. An average baby's body is 13.5 inches long and weighs around 32 ounces. Sunday comes and Saturday follows, the twenty-seventh week.

What Your Partner Might Experience This Week

At twenty-seven weeks, expecting moms may continue to experience symptoms like heartburn, leg cramps, forgetfulness, Braxton Hicks contractions, and vision changes. This week, your partner may notice increased breast size. She may develop hemorrhoids from straining during bowel movements.

Use the LOVE Compass to listen to your partner and observe her emotions and stress levels. Then, form your treasuring plan so she can feel your love and care for her and your baby.

"Love one another as I have loved you." John 13:34

This Week's Treasuring Plan

Each day this week, St. Joseph help me to be:

Loving • Joyful • Peaceful • Patient • Kind
• Generous • Faithful • Gentle • Self-Controlled

Strategy: Admire • Encourage • Appreciate

The Mary/St. Joseph songs I will listen to this week:	Any songs, pages 15-45

For My Life Partner

The Music I Am Making	What I Am Composing	Done
Daily Prayers	See pages 86-87.	
Finding Melody of Connection (Page 74)		
Writing Lyrics to Treasure (Page 75)		
Making Notation (Page 76)		
Rehearsing Your Love (Page 77)		
Performing in Person (Page 78)		

For My Unborn Baby

Affirming Action	What I Am Composing	Done
Daily Prayers	See pages 86-87.	
Words	See pages 111-114.	
Admiring Songs	Any song, pages 119-127.	
Encouraging Songs	My Baby's Lungs, page 132. Precious Baby, Use Your Lungs, page 136.	
Appreciating Songs	Any song, pages 139-147.	
Baby talk		

Weekly Journal

Dates: ________________

I Treasure God

I Treasure My Partner

"You formed my inmost being; you knit me in my mother's womb. I praise you, so wonderfully you have made me; wonderful are your works!" Psalm 139:13-14

Weekly Journal

Dates: ________________

I Treasure My Unborn Baby

I Treasure Me

Week 28

Your Baby Grows This Week

Then God whispers, "Let the baby get better using the gift of eyes." And so it happens. Your baby's eyes begin to move faster and more frequently. Your baby's brain tissue develops furrows and ridges so she/he will be able to remember, learn and think. An average baby is over 14 inches long and weighs around 42 ounces. Sunday comes and Saturday follows, the twenty-eighth week.

What Your Partner Might Experience This Week

At twenty-eight weeks, expecting moms may continue to experience symptoms like heartburn, leg cramps, forgetfulness, Braxton Hicks contractions, and vision changes. Aches and pains tend to increase. Your partner may experience greater back pain. She may have gained 19 pounds by this week, depending on the size of your baby and other factors.

Use the LOVE Compass to listen to your partner and observe her emotions and stress levels. Then, form your treasuring plan so she can feel your love and care for her and your baby.

"Love one another as I have loved you." John 13:34

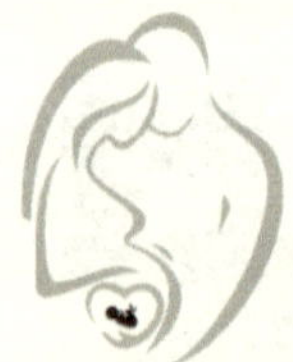

This Week's Treasuring Plan

Each day this week, St. Joseph help me to be:

Loving • Joyful • Peaceful • Patient • Kind • Generous • Faithful • Gentle • Self-Controlled

Strategy: Admire • Encourage • Appreciate

The Mary/St. Joseph songs I will listen to this week:	Any songs, pages 15-45

For My Life Partner

The Music I Am Making	What I Am Composing	Done
Daily Prayers	See pages 86-87.	
Finding Melody of Connection (Page 74)		
Writing Lyrics to Treasure (Page 75)		
Making Notation (Page 76)		
Rehearsing Your Love (Page 77)		
Performing in Person (Page 78)		

For My Unborn Baby

Affirming Action	What I Am Composing	Done
Daily Prayers	See pages 86-87.	
Words	See pages 111-114.	
Admiring Songs	Any song, pages 119-127.	
Encouraging Songs	Precious Baby, Blink Your Eyes, page 137.	
Appreciating Songs	Any song, pages 139-147.	
Baby talk		

Weekly Journal

Dates: ________________

I Treasure God

I Treasure My Partner

"You formed my inmost being; you knit me in my mother's womb. I praise you, so wonderfully you have made me; wonderful are your works!" Psalm 139:13-14

Weekly Journal

Dates: ____________________

I Treasure My Unborn Baby

____

____

____

____

____

____

____

____

____

I Treasure Me

____

____

____

____

____

____

____

____

____

Week 29

Your Baby Grows This Week

Then God whispers, "Let the gift of baby's skin develop and let his body grow stronger." And so it happens. Your baby's skin grows thicker, her bones grow harder, and his body adds more fat and muscle. An average baby's body is 14.75 inches long and weighs around three pounds or 48 ounces. Sunday comes and Saturday follows, the twenty-ninth week.

What Your Partner Might Experience This Week

At twenty-nine weeks, expecting moms may continue to experience symptoms like increased aches and pains, heartburn, leg cramps, forgetfulness, Braxton Hicks contractions, and vision changes. Your partner may experience the return of fatigue and lower energy now. She may have mild swelling in her ankles and feet.

Use the LOVE Compass to listen to your partner and observe her emotions and stress levels. Then, form your treasuring plan so she can feel your love and care for her and your baby.

"Love one another as I have loved you." John 13:34

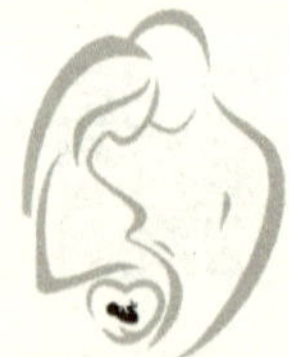

This Week's Treasuring Plan

Each day this week, St. Joseph help me to be:

Loving • Joyful • Peaceful • Patient • Kind
• Generous • Faithful • Gentle • Self-Controlled

Strategy: Admire • Encourage • Appreciate

The Mary/St. Joseph songs I will listen to this week:	Any songs, pages 15-45

For My Life Partner

The Music I Am Making	What I Am Composing	Done
Daily Prayers	See pages 86-87.	
Finding Melody of Connection (Page 74)		
Writing Lyrics to Treasure (Page 75)		
Making Notation (Page 76)		
Rehearsing Your Love (Page 77)		
Performing in Person (Page 78)		

For My Unborn Baby

Affirming Action	What I Am Composing	Done
Daily Prayers	See pages 86-87.	
Words	See pages 111-114.	
Admiring Songs	Any song, pages 119-127.	
Encouraging Songs	My Precious One, Month 7, page 134. Seven Months Now, page 138.	
Appreciating Songs	Any song, pages 139-147.	
Baby talk		

Weekly Journal

Dates: ________________

I Treasure God

___
___
___
___
___
___
___
___
___

I Treasure My Partner

___
___
___
___
___
___
___
___
___

"You formed my inmost being; you knit me in my mother's womb. I praise you, so wonderfully you have made me; wonderful are your works!" Psalm 139:13-14

Weekly Journal

Dates: ________________

I Treasure My Unborn Baby

____

____

____

____

____

____

____

____

____

I Treasure Me

____

____

____

____

____

____

____

____

____

Week 30

Your Baby Grows This Week

Then God whispers, "Let the baby strengthen its gift of breathing." And so it happens. You baby begins to hiccup and contract her/his muscles so that she/he can breathe more easily. An average baby's body is 15.25 inches long and weighs around 52 ounces. Sunday comes and Saturday follows, the thirtieth week.

What Your Partner Might Experience This Week

At thirty weeks, expecting moms may continue to experience symptoms like increased aches and pains, fatigue, swelling, heartburn, leg cramps, forgetfulness, Braxton Hicks contractions, and vision changes. Your partner may have great mood swings and need your support and affirming presence. She may be sensitive to developing carpal tunnel syndrome.

Use the LOVE Compass to listen to your partner and observe her emotions and stress levels. Then, form your treasuring plan so she can feel your love and care for her and your baby.

"Love one another as I have loved you." John 13:34

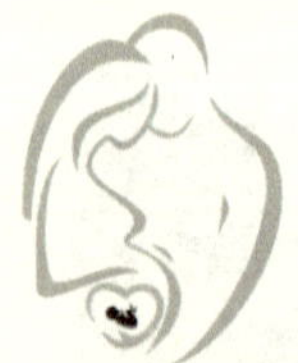

This Week's Treasuring Plan

Each day this week, St. Joseph help me to be:

Loving • Joyful • Peaceful • Patient • Kind • Generous • Faithful • Gentle • Self-Controlled

Strategy: Admire • Encourage • Appreciate

The Mary/St. Joseph songs I will listen to this week:	Any songs, pages 15-45

For My Life Partner

The Music I Am Making	What I Am Composing	Done
Daily Prayers	See pages 86-87.	
Finding Melody of Connection (Page 74)		
Writing Lyrics to Treasure (Page 75)		
Making Notation (Page 76)		
Rehearsing Your Love (Page 77)		
Performing in Person (Page 78)		

For My Unborn Baby

Affirming Action	What I Am Composing	Done
Daily Prayers	See pages 86-87.	
Words	See pages 111-114.	
Admiring Songs	Any song, pages 119-127.	
Encouraging Songs	Precious Baby, Use Your Lungs, page 136.	
Appreciating Songs	Any song, pages 139-147.	
Baby talk		

Weekly Journal

Dates: ________________

I Treasure God

I Treasure My Partner

"You formed my inmost being; you knit me in my mother's womb. I praise you, so wonderfully you have made me; wonderful are your works!" Psalm 139:13-14

Weekly Journal

Dates: ________________

I Treasure My Unborn Baby

____

____

____

____

____

____

____

____

____

I Treasure Me

____

____

____

____

____

____

____

____

____

Week 31

Your Baby Grows This Week

Then God whispers, "Let the baby blink its eyes and increase its rate of breathing." And so it happens. Your baby begins to blink his/her eyes and his/her breathing movements increase to one-third of the time. An average baby's body is 15.75 inches long and weighs around 60 ounces. Sunday comes and Saturday follows, the thirty-first week.

What Your Partner Might Experience This Week

At thirty-one weeks, expecting moms may continue to experience symptoms like increased aches and pains, fatigue, swelling, heartburn, leg cramps, forgetfulness, stronger Braxton Hicks contractions, mood swings, and vision changes. Your partner may develop "leaky breasts" as they prepare to make milk for your baby.

Use the LOVE Compass to listen to your partner and observe her emotions and stress levels. Then, form your treasuring plan so she can feel your love and care for her and your baby.

"Love one another as I have loved you." John 13:34

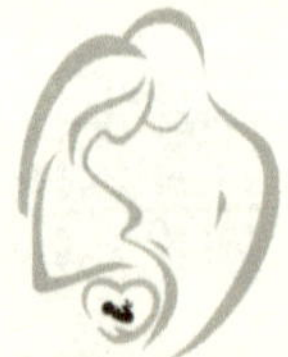

This Week's Treasuring Plan

Each day this week, St. Joseph help me to be:

Loving • Joyful • Peaceful • Patient • Kind • Generous • Faithful • Gentle • Self-Controlled

Strategy: Admire • Encourage • Appreciate

The Mary/St. Joseph songs I will listen to this week:	Any songs, pages 15-45

For My Life Partner

The Music I Am Making	What I Am Composing	Done
Daily Prayers	See pages 86-87.	
Finding Melody of Connection (Page 74)		
Writing Lyrics to Treasure (Page 75)		
Making Notation (Page 76)		
Rehearsing Your Love (Page 77)		
Performing in Person (Page 78)		

For My Unborn Baby

Affirming Action	What I Am Composing	Done
Daily Prayers	See pages 86-87.	
Words	See pages 111-114.	
Admiring Songs	Any song, pages 119-127.	
Encouraging Songs	Precious Baby, Use Your Lungs, page 136. Precious Baby, Blink Your Eyes, page 137.	
Appreciating Songs	Any song, pages 139-147.	
Baby talk		

Weekly Journal

Dates: ________________

I Treasure God

____

____

____

____

____

____

____

____

____

I Treasure My Partner

____

____

____

____

____

____

____

____

____

"You formed my inmost being; you knit me in my mother's womb. I praise you, so wonderfully you have made me; wonderful are your works!" Psalm 139:13-14

Weekly Journal

Dates: ________________

I Treasure My Unborn Baby

____

____

____

____

____

____

____

____

____

I Treasure Me

____

____

____

____

____

____

____

____

____

Week 32

Your Baby Grows This Week

Then God whispers, "Let the baby start to turn and rest." And so it happens. Your baby begins to turn head-down in Mom's womb, at his/her own pace. She/he begins to make time for sleep and being awake. An average baby's body is 16.25 inches long and weighs around 64 ounces. Sunday comes and Saturday follows, the thirty-second week.
This may be a good week to get your home ready for your baby's home coming: nursery, supplies, and more, if you haven't already.

What Your Partner Might Experience This Week

At thirty-two weeks, expecting moms may continue to experience symptoms like increased aches and pains, fatigue, swelling, stronger heartburn, leg cramps, forgetfulness, stronger Braxton Hicks contractions, mood swings, and vision changes. Your partner may feel a greater variety of your baby's movements inside her uterus.

Use the LOVE Compass to listen to your partner and observe her emotions and stress levels. Then, form your treasuring plan so she can feel your love and care for her and your baby.

"Love one another as I have loved you." John 13:34

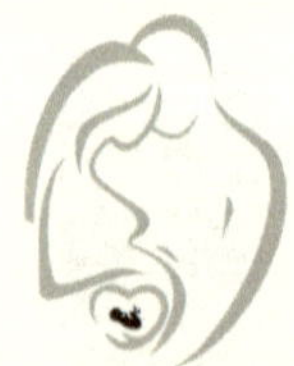

This Week's Treasuring Plan

Each day this week, St. Joseph help me to be:

Loving • Joyful • Peaceful • Patient • Kind
• Generous • Faithful • Gentle • Self-Controlled

Strategy: Admire • Encourage • Appreciate

The Mary/St. Joseph songs I will listen to this week:	Any songs, pages 15-45

For My Life Partner

The Music I Am Making	What I Am Composing	Done
Daily Prayers	See pages 86-87.	
Finding Melody of Connection (Page 74)		
Writing Lyrics to Treasure (Page 75)		
Making Notation (Page 76)		
Rehearsing Your Love (Page 77)		
Performing in Person (Page 78)		

For My Unborn Baby

Affirming Action	What I Am Composing	Done
Daily Prayers	See pages 86-87.	
Words	See pages 111-114.	
Admiring Songs	Any song, pages 119-127.	
Encouraging Songs	My Baby's Body Rests and Naps, page 132.	
Appreciating Songs	Any song, pages 139-147.	
Baby talk		

Weekly Journal

Dates: ________________

I Treasure God

I Treasure My Partner

"You formed my inmost being; you knit me in my mother's womb. I praise you, so wonderfully you have made me; wonderful are your works!" Psalm 139:13-14

Weekly Journal

Dates: ________________

I Treasure My Unborn Baby

I Treasure Me

Week 33

Your Baby Grows This Week

Then God whispers, "Let the baby practice eating." And so it happens. Your baby begins to coordinate sucking and swallowing so she/he can breastfeed after birth. Your baby's bones become fully developed. An average baby's body is nearly 17 inches long and weighs around 72 ounces. Sunday comes and Saturday follows, the thirty-third week.

Keep getting your home ready for your baby's homecoming: the nursery, furniture, supplies, and more. Don't wait until the last moment.

What Your Partner Might Experience This Week

At thirty-three weeks, expecting moms may continue to experience symptoms like increased aches and pains, fatigue, swelling, stronger heartburn, leg cramps, forgetfulness, stronger Braxton Hicks contractions, mood swings, and vision changes. Your partner may feel greater pain in her ribs and a shortness of breath.

Use the LOVE Compass to listen to your partner and observe her emotions and stress levels. Then, form your treasuring plan so she can feel your love and care for her and your baby.

"Love one another as I have loved you." John 13:34

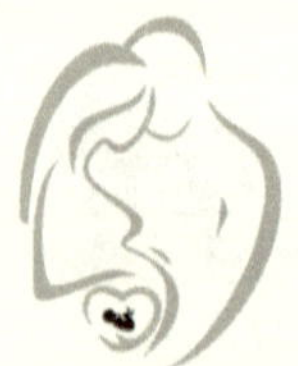

This Week's Treasuring Plan

Each day this week, St. Joseph help me to be:

Loving • Joyful • Peaceful • Patient • Kind • Generous • Faithful • Gentle • Self-Controlled

Strategy: Admire • Encourage • Appreciate

The Mary/St. Joseph songs I will listen to this week:	Any songs, pages 15-45

For My Life Partner

The Music I Am Making	What I Am Composing	Done
Daily Prayers	See pages 86-87.	
Finding Melody of Connection (Page 74)		
Writing Lyrics to Treasure (Page 75)		
Making Notation (Page 76)		
Rehearsing Your Love (Page 77)		
Performing in Person (Page 78)		

For My Unborn Baby

Affirming Action	What I Am Composing	Done
Daily Prayers	See pages 86-87.	
Words	See pages 111-114.	
Admiring Songs	Any song, pages 119-127.	
Encouraging Songs	Precious Baby, Learn to Eat, page 135.	
Appreciating Songs	Any song, pages 139-147.	
Baby talk		

Weekly Journal

Dates: ____________

I Treasure God

____

____

____

____

____

____

____

____

____

I Treasure My Partner

____

____

____

____

____

____

____

____

____

"You formed my inmost being; you knit me in my mother's womb. I praise you, so wonderfully you have made me; wonderful are your works!" Psalm 139:13-14

Weekly Journal

Dates: ________________

I Treasure My Unborn Baby

I Treasure Me

Week 34

Your Baby Grows This Week

Then God whispers, "Let the baby dance inside Mom." And so it happens. Your baby begins to move actively about in the amniotic fluid inside Mom's womb. An average baby's body is almost 18 inches long and weighs around 80 ounces. Sunday comes and Saturday follows, the thirty-fourth week.
Review with your partner what you need to make your home ready for your baby's homecoming: the nursery, furniture, supplies, and more.

What Your Partner Might Experience This Week

At thirty-four weeks, expecting moms may continue to experience symptoms like increased aches and pains, fatigue, swelling, stronger heartburn, leg cramps, forgetfulness, stronger Braxton Hicks contractions, mood swings, and vision changes. Your partner may have more frequent urination, and even leaking urine during this time.

Use the LOVE Compass to listen to your partner and observe her emotions and stress levels. Then, form your treasuring plan so she can feel your love and care for her and your baby.

"Love one another as I have loved you." John 13:34

This Week's Treasuring Plan

Each day this week, St. Joseph help me to be:

Loving • Joyful • Peaceful • Patient • Kind • Generous • Faithful • Gentle • Self-Controlled

Strategy: Admire • Encourage • Appreciate

The Mary/St. Joseph songs I will listen to this week:	Any songs, pages 15-45

For My Life Partner

The Music I Am Making	What I Am Composing	Done
Daily Prayers	See pages 86-87.	
Finding Melody of Connection (Page 74)		
Writing Lyrics to Treasure (Page 75)		
Making Notation (Page 76)		
Rehearsing Your Love (Page 77)		
Performing in Person (Page 78)		

For My Unborn Baby

Affirming Action	What I Am Composing	Done
Daily Prayers	See pages 86-87.	
Words	See pages 111-114.	
Admiring Songs	Any song, pages 119-127.	
Encouraging Songs	Precious Baby, Wiggle Toes, page 137. Eight Months Now, page 138.	
Appreciating Songs	Any song, pages 139-147.	
Baby talk		

Weekly Journal

Dates: ________________

I Treasure God

____

____

____

____

____

____

____

____

____

I Treasure My Partner

____

____

____

____

____

____

____

____

____

"You formed my inmost being; you knit me in my mother's womb. I praise you, so wonderfully you have made me; wonderful are your works!" Psalm 139:13-14

Weekly Journal

Dates: ________________

I Treasure My Unborn Baby

____

____

____

____

____

____

____

____

____

I Treasure Me

____

____

____

____

____

____

____

____

____

Week 35

Your Baby Grows This Week

Then God whispers, "Let the baby's brain grow." And so it happens. Your baby's brain begins to grow more rapidly. An average baby is about 20.5 inches long and weighs around 88 ounces. Sunday comes and Saturday follows, the thirty-fifth week.

Do a dry run of what your home will look like when your baby comes home. Ask your partner and friends what else you will need.

What Your Partner Might Experience This Week

At thirty-five weeks, expecting moms may continue to experience symptoms like increased urination, fatigue, swelling, stronger heartburn, leg cramps, forgetfulness, stronger Braxton Hicks contractions, and mood swings. Your partner may have more difficulty in sleeping and stronger headaches now.

Use the LOVE Compass to listen to your partner and observe her emotions and stress levels. Then, form your treasuring plan so she can feel your love and care for her and your baby.

"Love one another as I have loved you." John 13:34

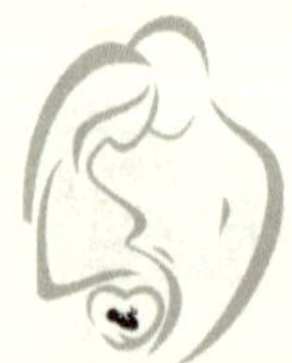

This Week's Treasuring Plan

Each day this week, St. Joseph help me to be:

Loving • Joyful • Peaceful • Patient • Kind • Generous • Faithful • Gentle • Self-Controlled

Strategy: Admire • Encourage • Appreciate

The Mary/St. Joseph songs I will listen to this week:	Any songs, pages 15-45

For My Life Partner

The Music I Am Making	What I Am Composing	Done
Daily Prayers	See pages 86-87.	
Finding Melody of Connection (Page 74)		
Writing Lyrics to Treasure (Page 75)		
Making Notation (Page 76)		
Rehearsing Your Love (Page 77)		
Performing in Person (Page 78)		

For My Unborn Baby

Affirming Action	What I Am Composing	Done
Daily Prayers	See pages 86-87.	
Words	See pages 111-114.	
Admiring Songs	Any song, pages 119-127.	
Encouraging Songs	Brain and Nerves Grow Rapidly, page 130.	
Appreciating Songs	Any song, pages 139-147.	
Baby talk		

Weekly Journal

Dates: ________________

I Treasure God

I Treasure My Partner

Weekly Journal

Dates: ________________

I Treasure My Unborn Baby

I Treasure Me

Week 36

Your Baby Grows This Week

Then God whispers, "Let the baby prepare for birth." And so it happens. Your baby's body drops lower in mom's abdomen and his/her blinking gets faster. An average baby's body is 20.5 inches long and weighs around 96 ounces. Sunday comes and Saturday follows, the thirty-sixth week.

Finalize what your home will look like when your baby comes home. Ask your partner and friends what else you will need.

What Your Partner Might Experience This Week

At thirty-six weeks, expecting moms may continue to experience symptoms like increased urination, fatigue, swelling, stronger heartburn, leg cramps, forgetfulness, stronger Braxton Hicks contractions, and mood swings. Your partner may experience "lightening" now (or later)-your baby is dropping lower in her pelvis, which gives her more room to breath.

Use the LOVE Compass to listen to your partner and observe her emotions and stress levels. Then, form your treasuring plan so she can feel your love and care for her and your baby.

"Love one another as I have loved you." John 13:34

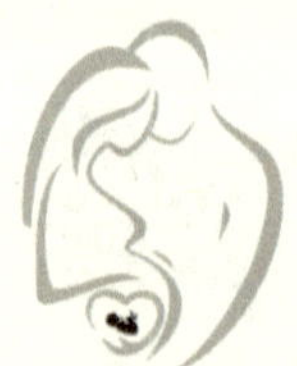

This Week's Treasuring Plan

Each day this week, St. Joseph help me to be:

Loving • Joyful • Peaceful • Patient • Kind
• Generous • Faithful • Gentle • Self-Controlled

Strategy: Admire • Encourage • Appreciate

The Mary/St. Joseph songs I will listen to this week:	Any songs, pages 15-45

For My Life Partner

The Music I Am Making	What I Am Composing	Done
Daily Prayers	See pages 86-87.	
Finding Melody of Connection (Page 74)		
Writing Lyrics to Treasure (Page 75)		
Making Notation (Page 76)		
Rehearsing Your Love (Page 77)		
Performing in Person (Page 78)		

For My Unborn Baby

Affirming Action	What I Am Composing	Done
Daily Prayers	See pages 86-87.	
Words	See pages 111-114.	
Admiring Songs	Any song, pages 119-127.	
Encouraging Songs	A Few Weeks Now, page 150. New Day to Rest and Turn, page 149.	
Appreciating Songs	Any song, pages 139-147.	
Baby talk		

Weekly Journal

Dates: ________________

I Treasure God

I Treasure My Partner

"You formed my inmost being; you knit me in my mother's womb. I praise you, so wonderfully you have made me; wonderful are your works!" Psalm 139:13-14

Weekly Journal

Dates: ________________

I Treasure My Unborn Baby

I Treasure Me

Week 37

Your Baby Grows This Week

Then God whispers, "Let the baby start to put on the finishing touches." And so it happens. Your baby's skin smooths out and his/her circulatory system completes its growth. An average baby's body is 20.5 inches long and weighs around 104 ounces. Sunday comes and Saturday follows, the thirty-seventh week.

What Your Partner Might Experience This Week

At thirty-seven weeks, expecting moms may continue to experience symptoms like increased urination, fatigue, swelling, stronger heartburn, leg cramps, forgetfulness, and stronger, more noticeable Braxton Hicks contractions. Your partner may discharge a mucus plug from her cervix.

Use the LOVE Compass to listen to your partner and observe her emotions and stress levels. Then, form your treasuring plan so she can feel your love and care for her and your baby.

"Love one another as I have loved you." John 13:34

This Week's Treasuring Plan

Each day this week, St. Joseph help me to be:

Loving • Joyful • Peaceful • Patient • Kind • Generous • Faithful • Gentle • Self-Controlled

Strategy: Admire • Encourage • Appreciate

The Mary/St. Joseph songs I will listen to this week:	Any songs, pages 15-45

For My Life Partner

The Music I Am Making	What I Am Composing	Done
Daily Prayers	See pages 86-87.	
Finding Melody of Connection (Page 74)		
Writing Lyrics to Treasure (Page 75)		
Making Notation (Page 76)		
Rehearsing Your Love (Page 77)		
Performing in Person (Page 78)		

For My Unborn Baby

Affirming Action	What I Am Composing	Done
Daily Prayers	See pages 86-87.	
Words	See pages 111-114.	
Admiring Songs	Any song, pages 119-127.	
Encouraging Songs	My Precious One, Month 9, page 138. My Baby's Heart, page 132.	
Appreciating Songs	Any song, pages 139-147.	
Baby talk		

Weekly Journal

Dates: ________________

I Treasure God

I Treasure My Partner

"You formed my inmost being; you knit me in my mother's womb. I praise you, so wonderfully you have made me; wonderful are your works!" Psalm 139:13-14

Weekly Journal

Dates: ________________

I Treasure My Unborn Baby

I Treasure Me

Week 38

Your Baby Rests This Week

Then God whispers, "Let the baby pause and rest." And so it happens. The downy hair on your baby's body begins to disappear, and his/her growth slows down. An average baby's body is about the same size as the week before–20.5 inches long and weighs around 104 ounces. Sunday comes and Saturday follows, the thirty-eighth week.

What Your Partner Might Experience This Week

At thirty-eight weeks, expecting moms may continue to experience symptoms like increased urination, fatigue, swelling, stronger heartburn, leg cramps, forgetfulness, and stronger, more noticeable Braxton Hicks contractions. Your partner may waddle when she walks because of your baby's position in her body. She may feel a little unstable or clumsy in her movements.

Use the LOVE Compass to listen to your partner and observe her emotions and stress levels. Then, form your treasuring plan so she can feel your love and care for her and your baby.

"Love one another as I have loved you." John 13:34

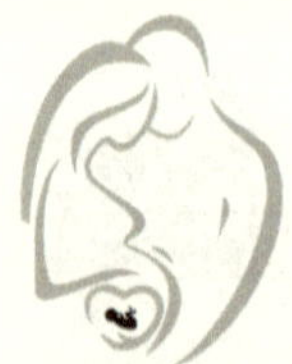

This Week's Treasuring Plan

Each day this week, St. Joseph help me to be:

Loving • Joyful • Peaceful • Patient • Kind • Generous • Faithful • Gentle • Self-Controlled

Strategy: Admire • Encourage • Appreciate

The Mary/St. Joseph songs I will listen to this week:	Any songs, pages 15-45

For My Life Partner

The Music I Am Making	What I Am Composing	Done
Daily Prayers	See pages 86-87.	
Finding Melody of Connection (Page 74)		
Writing Lyrics to Treasure (Page 75)		
Making Notation (Page 76)		
Rehearsing Your Love (Page 77)		
Performing in Person (Page 78)		

For My Unborn Baby

Affirming Action	What I Am Composing	Done
Daily Prayers	See pages 86-87.	
Words	See pages 111-114.	
Admiring Songs	Any song, pages 119-127.	
Encouraging Songs	My Baby's Body Rests and Naps, page 132. New Day to Rest and Turn, page 149.	
Appreciating Songs	Any song, pages 139-147.	
Baby talk		

Weekly Journal

Dates: ________________

I Treasure God

___

___

___

___

___

___

___

___

___

I Treasure My Partner

___

___

___

___

___

___

___

___

___

Weekly Journal

Dates: ________________

I Treasure My Unborn Baby

I Treasure Me

Week 39

Your Baby Gets Ready for Birth This Week

Then God whispers, "Let the baby admire its last days in its mother's womb." And so it happens. Your baby's lungs are fully ready to cry and breathe; his/her arm and leg muscles are strong; your baby's fingernails and toenails are complete. The downy hair on your baby's body disappears. An average baby's body is about the same size as the week before: 20.5 inches long and weighs around seven pounds. Sunday comes and Saturday follows, the thirty-ninth week.

What Your Partner Might Experience This Week

At thirty-nine weeks, expecting moms may continue to experience symptoms like increased urination, fatigue, swelling, stronger heartburn, leg cramps, forgetfulness, and stronger, more noticeable Braxton Hicks contractions. Your partner's body is getting ready for birth. She may experience dilation in her cervix and diarrhea as her hormones change.

Use the LOVE Compass to listen to your partner and observe her emotions and stress levels. Then, form your treasuring plan so she can feel your love and care for her and your baby.

"Love one another as I have loved you." John 13:34

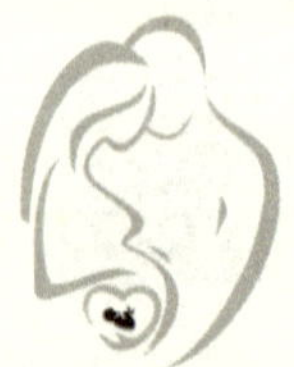

This Week's Treasuring Plan

Each day this week, St. Joseph help me to be:

Loving • Joyful • Peaceful • Patient • Kind
• Generous • Faithful • Gentle • Self-Controlled

Strategy: Admire • Encourage • Appreciate

The Mary/St. Joseph songs I will listen to this week:	Any songs, pages 15-45

For My Life Partner

The Music I Am Making	What I Am Composing	Done
Daily Prayers	See pages 86-87.	
Finding Melody of Connection (Page 74)		
Writing Lyrics to Treasure (Page 75)		
Making Notation (Page 76)		
Rehearsing Your Love (Page 77)		
Performing in Person (Page 78)		

For My Unborn Baby

Affirming Action	What I Am Composing	Done
Daily Prayers	See pages 86-87.	
Words	See pages 111-114.	
Admiring Songs	Any song, pages 119-127.	
Encouraging Songs	God is Bringing You to Birth, page 151. New Day to Rest and Turn, page 149.	
Appreciating Songs	Any song, pages 139-147.	
Baby talk		

Weekly Journal

Dates: ________________

I Treasure God

I Treasure My Partner

"You formed my inmost being; you knit me in my mother's womb. I praise you, so wonderfully you have made me; wonderful are your works!" Psalm 139:13-14

Weekly Journal

Dates: ________________

I Treasure My Unborn Baby

____

____

____

____

____

____

____

____

____

I Treasure Me

____

____

____

____

____

____

____

____

____

Week 40

Your Baby Is Ready for Birth This Week

Then God said, "Let the baby be born and come into the light of the world!" And so it happens. Your baby's body moves from Mom's womb to live outside. Your baby enters the world, ready to eat, cry, breathe, and kick. Welcome, little one! Your baby completes the first major journey of life. Sunday comes and Saturday follows, the fortieth week.
This is it! Your baby is coming home. Make sure all your preparations for your baby's space are ready.

What Your Partner Might Experience This Week

At forty weeks, most expecting moms are full-term and the baby is ready for birth. Your partner's body and actual delivery date will vary. She will experience active labor, which is the time when you must get her to the birthing center you have chosen. Her labor can last anywhere from 20 minutes to several hours. Your presence during delivery and birth is a precious gift to her.

Use the LOVE Compass to listen to your partner and observe her emotions and stress levels. Then, form your treasuring plan so she can feel your love and care for her and your baby.

"Love one another as I have loved you." John 13:34

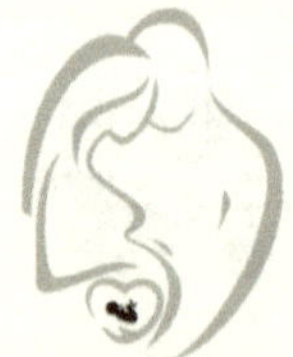

This Week's Treasuring Plan

Each day this week, St. Joseph help me to be:

Loving • Joyful • Peaceful • Patient • Kind • Generous • Faithful • Gentle • Self-Controlled

Strategy: Admire • Encourage • Appreciate

The Mary/St. Joseph songs I will listen to this week:	Any songs, pages 15-45

For My Life Partner

The Music I Am Making	What I Am Composing	Done
Daily Prayers	See pages 86-87.	
Finding Melody of Connection (Page 74)		
Writing Lyrics to Treasure (Page 75)		
Making Notation (Page 76)		
Rehearsing Your Love (Page 77)		
Performing in Person (Page 78)		

For My Unborn Baby

Affirming Action	What I Am Composing	Done
Daily Prayers	See pages 86-87.	
Words	See pages 111-114.	
Admiring Songs	Any song, pages 119-127.	
Encouraging Songs	God is Bringing You to Birth, page 151. Any Day Now, page 150.	
Appreciating Songs	Any song, pages 139-147.	
Baby talk		

Weekly Journal

Dates: ________________

I Treasure God

I Treasure My Partner

"You formed my inmost being; you knit me in my mother's womb. I praise you, so wonderfully you have made me; wonderful are your works!" Psalm 139:13-14

Weekly Journal

Dates: ________________

I Treasure My Unborn Baby

I Treasure Me

Giving Birth

Congratulations! You and your partner are ready to help your precious baby be born

Treasuring your partner and unborn child during and after birth are the last steps you take on the pregnancy journey. You've done the hard work of loving your baby with your partner during the many weeks of pregnancy. Now, it's time for your baby to leave your partner's womb and enter the world as your newborn.

The birth journey is unique for every family. Your doctor can offer you different options for the type of birth practice that fits your partner's medical situation. Discuss which options are healthy for your partner and your baby.

The Association of Prenatal and Perinatal Psychology and Health (APPPAH) studies pregnancy. In March 2023, the organization sponsored a webinar series for Birth Psychology Month. The series taught compassionate birth practices for a peaceful world. (A recording of the event is available at https://apppah.org.) Your baby's birth experience will have a profound effect on her/his life. Choose wisely.

If you wish and are able, you may continue the practice of speaking and singing loving words and songs to your baby as you and your partner get ready for delivery and birthing. The birthing time is a precious time for working together with your partner and baby in the most intimate way. Your presence during your baby's birth is a precious time. If you are willing and able to witness your child's birth, the birth experience will be even more special.

The next part of this journal section includes pages to write about your birthing experience, memories, thoughts, and feelings after your baby is born. Capture your first thoughts and memories. Write down a few words as you feel. Pages 152-158 contain treasuring songs for giving birth and welcoming your newborn baby.

Make this treasury a keepsake of memories for your pregnancy journey and birth that you may gift to your child when she/he is ready. When that time comes, write a letter to your child using the *My Gifting Letter to You* on page 3 of this book.

Date: ________________

I Treasure God

____

____

____

____

I Treasure My Partner

____

____

____

____

I Treasure My Unborn Baby

____

____

____

____

I Treasure Me

____

____

____

____

Date: ______________

My Precious Birth Memories

Date: ______________

My Precious Birth Memories

Date: ______________

My First Day with Baby

Research & Resources

Growing Positive Emotions

Your unborn child thrives when your partner holds positive, loving feelings as long as possible. Every human experience evokes a feeling that lasts or fades. That feeling's power depends on how much energy we give it. You have the power of choice. You can choose to have positive feelings or hold on to negative feelings. Positive feelings lead to growth; the opposite happens for negative feelings.

A feeling is just a feeling, nothing more. You can train your brain to think and hold positive thoughts and images and discard negative ones. Over time, you create a habit of visualizing, talking to yourself and thinking in positive ways.

One small way to do this is called "The Maui Effect," offered by Dr. BJ Fogg in his book, Tiny Habits.[25] When you get out of bed in the morning, put both feet flat on the floor and say, "It's going to be a great day."

Leaders in positive psychology offer resources and methods to build more conscious and intentional positivity in one's mind and heart. One practice is to meditate on loving-kindness taught by Dr. Barbara L. Fredrickson, professor of psychology at The University of North Carolina, Chapel Hill.

Her book, *Positivity: Discover the Upward Spiral That Will Change Your Life*,[26] offers many good ways to increase positivity and decrease negativity in your life. She describes ten positive emotions to focus on: joy, gratitude, serenity, interest, hope, pride, amusement, inspiration, awe, and love.

Imagine how richer your life might be–and how healthy your unborn child would be–if you invested a little time to nurture these positive emotions daily.

To learn more online, you can enroll in Dr. Fredrickson's free eleven-hour online course on positive psychology at coursera. org/learn/positive-psychology. The course offers skills in gratitude, kindness, meditation, and positive psychology.

A Stronger Partner Relationship

Love binds people together. A strong family is full of peace and joy. Negative emotions, apathy, or abuse weaken a family.

Love starts when you communicate with respect. Positive feelings, thoughts, and intentions help. During a pregnancy, two partners create an environment that affects themselves and others. A strong relationship needs your attention, presence, and purpose. Be present. Listen to your partner and share your own self.

The LOVE Compass

The LOVE Compass, described on pages 61-72, is a helpful tool to share care, concern, and understanding with one another. Remember, the LOVE Compass has a heart at the center as the pointing device.

Four movements guide the heart: Listen, Observe, Value, and Express. Valuing your partner means accepting her and using the treasuring process to admire, encourage, and appreciate her. The last movement of the LOVE Compass is to Express your care. Yet, your partner has a unique way that she experiences the love you are expressing. Her natural preference may differ from the way you experience love.

The 5 Love Languages®

Dr. Gary Chapman, a pastor and author, discovered five unique ways that love is expressed. In his 5 Love Languages® books, Dr. Chapman explains five different languages that men and women speak for love. Those five languages are physical touch, quality time, words of affirmation, receiving gifts, and acts of service.

The treasuring words and songs in this book fall into 'words of affirmation' category. You and your partner may be more expressive in one of the love languages than the other four love languages. Find out which love language is the strongest for you by completing a free online quiz at 5lovelanguages.com/quizzes.

This web page has two other quizzes: your language of apology and how well you handle anger. Making apologies and handling anger are keys for a healthy relationship.

Dr. Gary Chapman's signature book is very readable, *The 5 Love Languages: The Secret to Love That Lasts.* ® It is easy to read and contains sound instruction.

Happy Together: Building on Your Strengths
Suzann and James Pawelski are positive psychologists. They teach three strategies. The first is to build upon and affirm each other's strengths. Next, savor each other. Third, practice gratitude. Their book, *Happy Together: Using the Science of Positive Psychology to Build Love That Lasts*, shows readers how to cultivate an emotional connection with their partners.

The Gottman Institute
Dr. John Gottman has helped more than a million couples around the world build a stronger relationship and handle conflict. Check out their course, *Bringing Baby Home.* Learn more at https://gottmanconnect.com/couples.

Praying Together: My 3 Strands for Marriage
The concept of 3 Strands applies to partner relationships. Each relationship includes three persons: God, yourself, and another person. The My 3 Strands prayer for Marriage offers a way to remember and pray for each other. Please say the prayer as you wish.

A man and woman, with God's hands,
Knit a marriage of 3 strands.
Three cords of love, faith and hope
Weave a stronger bond than rope.
One greater love, a braid of three,
Formed by God, my spouse and me.
May my 3 strands be lifelong friends
With happiness, that never ends.
Counseling Support

If there is verbal, physical, or emotional abuse or rejection in your life, get help. Now that you are expecting, three lives matter: your partner, you and your baby. Decide to stand up for yourself. Contact your local church or community support hotline for referrals to qualified professionals.

Stress Reduction Resources

Constant, overwhelming stress during pregnancy is harmful to your partner's health and the health of your baby. The March of Dimes website has an excellent summary article at marchofdimes.org/find-support/topics/pregnancy/stress-and-pregnancy.

If you or your partner need relief from ongoing anxiety, depression, and negative emotions, there are many qualified professionals who can help. This may involve counseling, therapy, or other forms of professional treatment. Check with your local church or community support hotline for referrals.

Self-Help (Non-Medical) Programs
The Sedona Method involves a series of releasing questions you ask yourself to release and let go of unwanted, painful, or stressful feelings. The Sedona organization offers coaching and retreats. Learn more at sedona.com.

The Trilogy Codes by Dr. Alex Loyd offers a three-minute energy healing method to release stress, and heal emotions, and trauma that is easy to learn and do. Dr. Loyd offers home study versions, along with custom coaching. You can learn more at: /www.dralexanderloyd.com/trilogy/.

Mental Health Apps, include those stress-relieving techniques using your mobile phone. For a list reviewed by the American Institute of Stress, visit stress.org/mental-health-apps.

EFT (Emotional Freedom Technique–Tapping) is a mind-body method of tapping on acupuncture points on the face, hands, and body to resolve emotional issues. There are several practitioners who teach tapping. A popular site with a variety of applications is thetappingsolution.com.

Prayers for inner peace and harmony help reduce stress. The resting prayer on page 87 offers a peaceful way to relax and get calm when you feel stressed.

Healing Your Inner Unborn Child

If you experienced any trauma when you were in your mother's womb or during birth, I am sorry. That is a heavy burden that you've carried for years. There is hope for you. If your mother or father did not love or want you before or after you were born, please know that God has always wanted and loved you. You are lovely. You are loving. You are beloved. No matter what gender, size, skin color, race, economic class, or creed.

Your Emotional Health is Important for Your Child
You are not alone. It is not your fault. Your parents are not perfect, yet you survived to read this page. The book, *Tomorrow's Baby*, by Dr. Thomas Verny, M.D., outlines how unhappy children's lives become when their mothers feel unloved or unwanted and pass unhealed memories to their unborn children. Those children may turn to drugs, crime, and other unhealthy behaviors looking for the love they missed in pregnancy, childbirth, and early childhood.

You cannot change the past. God can heal the stressful memories, negative emotions, images, or beliefs you have about yourself. It is God's business and delight to make you whole and restore your life. God will give you the wisdom and grace to love and want your unborn child.

The first step is to recognize that you've suffered trauma. Then, decide to seek healing. Healing is very possible and likely. Healing is a process that takes time. A small scrape needs a band-aid and protection so that the blood will stop and the skin will grow back healthy again in a matter of days. A deeper injury takes longer to heal. That is okay. What matters is that you're taking care of yourself and your unborn child to live a better and healthier life.

Find Healing Options
There are qualified counselors, psychologists, psychotherapists, and psychiatrists who specialize in prenatal and birth trauma. The preferred professionals to consult with specialize in birth psychology. Ask your doctor for referrals.

The Association for Prenatal and Perinatal Psychology and Health (APPPAH) is the leading U.S. Professional group for emotional health during pregnancy. The association offers online courses to learn about nurturing during pregnancy.

Dr. Alex Loyd, founder of the LT3 and Trilogy Codes, offers a relatively painless, quick, and proven way to release the stress of past traumas and memories, using a combination of healing energy techniques and prayer. Dr. Loyd formulated a trio of energy "codes" for healing specific issues with mom, dad, siblings, God, and others that might have occurred when you were in your mother's womb, during birth, or early childhood. You can learn more at dralexanderloyd.com/trilogy.

Ask the "Saints in Your Corner" Prayer Circle for Healing
God's love and power to heal and restore people are at the heart of all successful and lasting healing. Your prayer circle can pray for you. Mary, the Mother of Jesus, prays for you. Just ask.

Invite the saints to pray for you. They are very willing to serve as members of your prayer circle. Google their prayers or novenas.

St. Joseph, the husband of Mary and stepfather of Jesus, is the patron saint and protector of families. He cared for Mary while she was expecting Jesus. He cares for your family too. Read more about St. Joseph on pages 88-94.

St. Gerard Majella is the patron saint of expecting mothers who can pray for you. You can learn more from the website, themotherssaint.org, or the Facebook group at www.facebook.com/saintgerardmajella.

St. Anne, the mother of Mary and grandmother of Jesus, has a novena for expecting moms.

St. Gianna Beretta Molla, a 20th-century physician, wife, and mother, is a patron saint of unborn children and pregnant women. Learn more at saintgianna.org.

Many churches have prayer groups that will pray for you by name or anonymously. Those churches often have a prayer intention book in their narthex (lobby) where you or a friend can write your prayer intention for healing and health.

Coping and Hoping With Loss

Loss hurts. Loss triggers many negative emotions: pain, grief, mourning, depression, and sadness. Loss brings stress. Psychologists rank the death of a loved one as the number one source of stress in life. Coping with stress when someone dies is a process of recovery. Hoping after loss is a part of that journey.

Coping With Stress

Death is a part of life. We are all human beings. Our lives on earth are mortal and death is the doorway to the next life. Mourning and grief are natural when a loved one dies. The grief journey is unique for each person and each situation. The common experience is a wide range of emotions that can be intense and even devastating.

Grieving can produce constant negative emotions that can cause harm to you and your baby. If you experience the loss of a loved one, loss of health, a job, or another severe trial, get help. You need the support and love of friends and family. There are certified grief educators and professional grief counselors who can provide help, understanding, and guidance.

Don't go through grief alone; you need the support of your treasuring community. Methods like the Sedona Method, EFT, the Trilogy Codes, and others can provide relief from stress. An excellent source of information about grieving is in the books and on the website of David Kessler. Visit David's website at www.grief.com. At the time of this writing, he offers a free online course for bereaved parents at www.davidkesslertraining.com/parents.

Stephen Ministries offers a series of four easy-to-read books, *Journeying Through Grief.* Some churches have a Stephen Ministry with trained companions who can listen to you when you need a friend during the grieving process. You can learn more at stephenministries.org.

Hoping After Loss

Hope and peace are spiritual gifts of the Holy Spirit, which are yours for the asking. Without hope, it is easy to fall into a dark depression and despair for a long time. There is a difference between fleeting negative emotions and constant ones. Unborn babies are resilient to fleeting negative emotions but are vulnerable to constant negativity.

Ask for help. Spiritual counseling and prayer are resources that can help you reach acceptance and understand the meaning of loss. Find an experienced pastor or spiritual friend you can trust. Your prayer circle, including the prayers of Mary, is with you when a loss occurs.

It is beyond this book to provide detailed instructions and guidance when someone you love dies. I offer you my deepest condolences and prayers. I realize I may never meet you in person. I pray daily for the readers of this book, and that includes you.

If you would like a journal for a lost son or daughter, consider the *Treasured in My Heart: Talking, Singing, and Writing to You Loved One in Paradise* series, available on Amazon.com. Scan the QR code to learn more:

In Chapter 13 of his First Letter to the Corinthians, St. Paul writes that the three things that last are faith, hope, and love. Hope is the middle strand that unites faith and love. The greatest of the three strands is love. Love lasts for eternity–the last strand that never breaks–because God is love.

My 3 Strands for Eternity

A deceased loved one in God's hands
lives the fullness of 3 strands.
Three cords of love, faith and hope
weave a stronger bond than rope:
One lasting love, a braid of three,
God, my deceased ones and me.
May these 3 strands unite as one
at home with God when time is done.

Pregnancy Information Online

If you like to browse the Internet or your mobile phone, you can find recent and timely information about what happens in pregnancy. Look for established, authoritative sites that have reputable content, without getting smothered with advertising.

Here are several the most popular and reputable resources, in no particular order, as of the time of publication of this book. Feel free to visit them, read through the content, and pick the sites that resonate with you.

Websites

Fathers for Good	fathersforgood.org
Faithful Fathers	faithfulfathering.org
National Fatherhood Initiative	fatherhood.org
Parents.com	parents.com/pregnancy
Very Well Family	verywellfamily.com
WebMD Pregnancy	webmd.com/baby
What to Expect	whattoexpect.com

Pregnancy Blogs

All Pro Dad	allprodad.com
Child and Family Blog	childandfamilyblog.com
Fathercraft	fathercraft.com/blog
Fatherly	fatherly.com
Pregnancy Magazine	pregnancymagazine.com

Pregnancy Apps

Use your mobile phone with your pregnancy. Some have detailed graphics, 3D interactions, baby hand and foot sizes, fetal size comparisons, and more. List compiled by Parents Magazine (parents.com, updated March 2023.)

Contraction Timer

Daddy Up

Hi Daddy

Pregnant Dad

ProDaddy

The Big Daddy

WebMD Pregnancy (free)
What to Expect

Who's Your Daddy?

YouTube Video Channels

Dad University
youtube.com/@DadUniversity

Dad Verb
youtube.com/@dadverb

Focus on the Family
youtube.com/@focusonthefamily

The Doctors Bjorkman
youtube.com/@TheDoctorsBjorkman

Notes

1. Page 49. A layperson's explanation of Stage 1, Infancy, may be found at verywellmind.com/erik-eriksons-stages-of-psychosocial-development-2795740

2. Page 50. Review the books of Dr. Thomas Verny, MD and the psychologists' writings published through the Association of Prenatal and Perinatal Psychology and Health (APPPAH.) See the *Further Reading* section.

3. Page 50. Cellular memories are discussed in *Tomorrows' Baby* (pp. 153-158) and *The Embodied Mind* (pp. 85-88) by Dr. Thomas R. Verny, MD.

4. Page 50. *Holy Moments*, Matthew Kelly, pp. 54-55.

5. Page 50. *The Power of Moments*, Chip Heath & Dan Heath, pp. 12-16.

6. Page 52. Tiny habits are like "baby steps" and are fully described in the book *Tiny Habits, BJ Fogg*

7. Page 53. Gospel of Matthew 2:1-11.

8. Page 59. Ecclesiastes 4:2.

9. Page 62. God creating humanity in the Divine Image and Likeness is referenced in Genesis 1:27.

10. Page 62. Genesis 1:31.

11. Page 73. The following content is based on the book The 5 Love Languages: The Secret to Love that Lasts by Dr. Gary Chapman ©2015, Moody Publishers.

12. Page 80, *The Secret Life of the Unborn Child*, Verny, p. 49

13. Page 84. Gospel of Matthew 6:8.

14. Page 88. Read the stories of Joseph in Gospel of Matthew, Chapters 1 and 2.

15. Page 89, St. Paul's Letter to the Galatians 5:22-23

16. Page 93, confer Book of the Prophet Micah 6:8

17. Page 93, refer to Donald Calloway's book, *Consecration to St. Joseph* or check out the *Hallow* prayer app for the consecration series led by Fr. Mike Schmitz and Sr. Miriam James Heidland, SOLT.

18. Page 95. Mary's song of praise, The Magnificat, also known as The Canticle of Mary, is found in Luke 1:46-55.

18. Page 95. Refer to *Am I Not Your Mother: Reflections on Our Lady of Guadalupe*, Martinez, Magnificat, Inc.

20. Page 96. Confer the reflection for May 22, Gate of Heaven, *365 Mary*, Koenig-Bricker. This book also contains several daily reflections about Mary's pregnancy and motherhood.

21. Page 107. Gospel of John, 14:12

22. Page 116. *The Secret Life of the Unborn Child, Verny and Kelly, pages 22-23, 38-39.* See also *Nurturing the Unborn Child, Verny and Weintraub* for a month-by-month list of gentle music.

23. Page 164. The typical weekly development of an unborn child in the Weekly pages, excerpted from the pregnancy sections of verywellfamily.com and webmd.com websites. The actual development of your child may be faster or slower, depending on your pregnancy.

24. Page 172. Chapter 1 of the Book of Genesis is of the Priestly Tradition, in which God speaks each part of creation into existence. Chapter 2 depicts a God who "rolls up the sleeves" and mixed mud to make human beings.

25. Page 324. The "Maui Effect" is described in the Introduction section of *Tiny Habits,* BJ Fogg.

26. Page 324. Kindle version- *Positivity: Discover the Upward Spiral That Will Change Your Life*, Frederickson, Harmony Books

Further Reading

Here are several books that provide more in-depth information about positive emotions and love during the pregnancy journey. If you have the time and interest, read these books to gain additional information and wisdom. (For a more extensive list, visit Amazon.com and search for books in the Pregnancy & Childbirth category.)

Pregnancy

Chamberlain, David (2013), Windows to the Womb: Revealing the Conscious Baby from Conception to Birth, North Atlantic Books

Flanagan, Geraldine Lux (1965), The First Nine Months of Life: The Baby's Development from Conception through Birth," Simon & Schuster

Kulp, Adrian (2018, We're Pregnant! The First Time Dad's Pregnancy Handbook, Rockridge Press

Murkoff, Heidi (2016), What to Expect When You Are Expecting, 5th Edition, Workman Publishing Company

Nero, John (2021) The Pregnancy Guide for Men, Independent

Verny, Thomas R, PhD, Kelly, John (1981), The Secret Life the the Unborn Child, Dell Publishing Co. Inc.

Verny, Thomas R. M.D. and Weintraub, Pamela (2000), Nurturing the Unborn Child: A Nine Month Program for Soothing, Stimulating, and Communicating with Your Baby, Olmstead Press

Verny, Thomas R. M.D. and Weintraub Pamela (2002), Tomorrow's Baby: The Art and Science of Parenting from Conception through Infancy, Simon & Schuster

Building Positive Emotions

Dyer, Judy PhD (2023), "The Power of Emotions," Kindle Direct Publishing

Frederickson, Barbara L, PhD, (2013), Positivity: Discover the Upward Spiral That Will Change Your Life, Harmony Books

Frederickson, Barbara L, PhD (2013), Love 2.0: Creating Happiness and

Health in Moments of Connection, Plume

Memories and Moments

Chapman, Gary (2015), 5 Love Languages: The Secret to Love That Lasts®, Northfield Publishing

Chapman, Gary (2015), Anger: Taming a Powerful Emotion, Northfield Publishing

Clear, James (2018), Atomic Habits, Penguin

Ferrucci, Piero (2007), The Power of Kindness: The Unexpected Benefits of Living a Compassionate Life, Penguin Books, 2007

Fogg, BJ PhD (2019), Tiny Habits: The Small Changes That Change Everything, Harvest Publishing

Heath, Chip and Dan Heath (2017), The Power of Moments, Simon & Schuster

Kelly, Matthew (2022), Holy Moments: A Handbook for the Rest of Your Life, Blue Sparrow

St. Joseph, Father and Worker

Braudrick, Wayne and Mikeska, Jeremy (2022) Faithful Father: A Study of Joseph, Stone Tower Press

Calloway MIC, Donald H. (2019) Consecration to St. Joseph: The Wonders of Our Spiritual Father, Marian Press

Calloway MIC, Donald H. (2018) St. Joseph Gems: Daily Wisdom on Our Spiritual Father, Marian Press

DeLorenzo, Leonard J. (2021), Model of Faith: Reflecting on the Litany of Saint Joseph, Our Sunday Visitor Publishing Division

Hicks OSB, Fr. Boniface (2021), Through the Heart of St. Joseph, Emmaus Road Publishing

Kauth, Matthew (2022) The Imitation of St. Joseph, TAN Books

Perotta, Louise (2021) St. Joseph, Tender Father: His Life and Care for Us Today, Word Among Us Press

Pope Francis (2021), Patris Corde: With a Father's Heart, Our Sunday Visitor

Sarkasian, Rick (2004), Not Your Average Joe, Lifework Press

Winter, Ken (2021), A Carpenter Called Joseph, WildernessLessons

Acknowledgments

I have so many people to acknowledge and thank for the inspiration and encouragement during the writing of this work Many are named below, and there are so many more people who have touched my life directly through personal contact, so many more through their writing, talks, and witness of life, whose names are not listed here. Thank you, everyone!

None of this writing would have occurred without the grace and prayers of those special people praying for me, especially Mary and Joseph, Mother and earthly father of Jesus, those deceased family and friends in the Communion of Saints.

To my wonderful wife Cheryl of 40+ years, our daughter Emily who came into our lives when we were in our 40's–I love and treasure you. To my parents, Joel and Cecilia Pipitone, my grandparents Thomas and Lenora, Frank and Mary, aunts and uncles, my siblings Kathy (John) Martin, Gary (Sue), Mary Lynn (Lyle Rasmussen), Paul (Mary), and Jeff, our Parochka and Libera cousins, thank you for sharing your love presence with me.

To the two people who inspired me with the concept of Living Epiphany, Fr. Patrick J. Brennan and Dawn Mayer.

To the many "Joes" in my life, including my dad Joel, his cousins the two Joe Pepitones, Frs. Joe Kierce, Joe McGowan, Joe Kruszinki, and many more.

To the many people who inspired me with their witness of committed marriage and family life, including Tom and Pat Bouton, Tim and Charlene Kryszak, and so many more.

To people of good faith in parishes and churches, in the streets and in the pews, to my friends, brothers and the witness of Knights of Columbus for the unborn, and other pro-life organizations.

Most of all, the glory goes to God, our Heavenly Father, His Son Jesus, and the Holy Spirit, the source of all treasuring love.

About the Composers

Dave Pipitone composed the score of this book for you with inspiration from the Holy Spirit. As parents, you and your partner are co-conducting the chorus of creation. The words, songs, and music of your love serve to cherish and invite your unborn child to God's majestic, forever concert.

Dave is a Catholic husband, father, writer, and retired marketing professional for a non-profit Catholic organization. He owns Transforming Life Press, LLC, a publisher of inspirational/spiritual books in Poinciana, Florida. He has served as lector at Catholic parishes for more than 40 years, is a Vincentian member of The Society of St. Vincent de Paul and a Knight of Columbus.

Emma Bennett and her team produced the Mary and Joseph songs on pages 15-45. Emma is a professional singer, musician, and music producer from London, England with songs published on Spotify, iTunes/Apple Music, and iHeartRadio.com. Her five 'Concert in a Book' books, *The Journey of Love: Christian Songs for Marriage, America's Promise*, *Come to the Concert*, *Yearning for the Treasures of Heaven,* and *Unlimited Praise* are available on Amazon.com. Emma's songs are in the books, *Mary's Love Songs to Expecting Moms, The Concert Day,* and *Reveille for Eternity.* Her newest album, '*The Journey of Faith* is available online.

Charles Kyros, Curtis Leonard, Hazel Charles and Shalom Vereen are members of Emma's music production team, which has sung and produced songs for a variety of music genres and customers. You can contact Emma and her team through the website: www.singyourmusic.com

The vocals for the Treasuring Songs on pages 119-158 were performed by Melissa Altamirano of Haines City, FL accompanied by her son, Riccardo on guitar; the songs were recorded in Emmitt Burden's SpaceApe Studio in Haines City, FL.

Appendix: Legacy Songs

Blessing Prayer

This legacy song is about the nature of loving others–wishing the best of God's blessings and grace for their lives, and doing your best to bring those blessings about as you share life with others

Treasuring Lyrics

May the wings of faith mount up in you.
May the threat of fear fly far from you.
May you know God's might, bring safety in your sight,
May you reach God's height of love for you.
May your sins be whitened like the snow.
May your gaze be brightened by God's glow.
May God's pardon reach, may God's wisdom teach,
May God's grace give each the power to grow.

Refrain:
May the love of God abide in you.
May the dawn of praise arise in you.
May your heart rejoice, receive a blessing choice;
May you hear God's voice alive in you.
May you hear God's voice alive in you.

May God's people dance when they meet you.
May your vision glance a dream that's new.
Hands we join as one, give thanks for what's begun,
May God's Reign become a sign for you.
May the song of hope be sung in you.
May the wrongs of hate turn right and true.
May you make wars cease, as you share God's peace,
May your foes believe the Christ in you.

May you rest secure at long's day end.
May Jesus endure as your best friend.
May you see God's face, may you taste God's embrace,
May your banquet place sound an Amen.
May the gift of joy fill all your days.
May you lift up God with thanks and praise.
May the Spirit shine, in radiance divine,
Blossom like a vine in the Son's rays.

Scan the QR Code to listen on SoundCloud.com

Forever a Family

This legacy song is about the beauty of God's forever family, that starts in pregnancy. Listen to this song for inspiration about how your family is part of God's family. (Sung by Rihanna Curtis.)

Treasuring Lyrics

We're forever a fam'ly, we're born of God's grace.
We join hands as children from each land and race.
We believe in God's promise that all will be one.
We're a family together, united by love.

The child we're expecting, is hidden from sight.
Growing in darkness, yet bathed in God's light.
Our baby waits with us, until new birth takes place:
Keep our family together, let us see Your face. *Refrain.*

We sit at one table; we eat of one bread.
Our hope is in Jesus, by Him we are fed.
We'll dine at one banquet when day's end is done:
Knead your fam'ly together, unite us in love. *Refrain.*

We're adopted and grafted into Jesus the Vine.
As branches that bear fruit, we become God's wine.
That flows in abundance from a blessing cup:
Drink as fam'ly together, united by love. *Refrain.*

Our lives are in God's hands, we live day by day.
We bear every challenge with hope as we pray:
May we feed our wonder of life in the womb,
So that one day, our child will be born and bloom. *Refrain.*

So, let's join forever to give thanks and praise.
The God of all loving, through wonderful ways,
Has made us a people where each one belongs,
We're a fam'ly together, united by love. *Refrain.*

Scan the QR Code to listen on SoundCloud.com

Las Rosas de Maria

This legacy song deserves a more detailed explanation and background. The message and treasuring lyrics have a special meaning for you during the pregnancy journey.

The Blessed Virgin Mary, the mother of Jesus, appeared to Juan Diego, a poor native Indian, near Mexico City in December 1531. It was a time of great oppression of the native people.

The Lady told him to ask the local bishop to build a church in her honor on that spot. The bishop was skeptical and refused.

After several appearances, the Lady asked him to climb a barren hilltop and pick flowers. Juan Diego did so and found roses blooming in December. He went back to the Lady and gave her the roses, which she arranged in his tilma (cloak.) Then he bundled the roses up to keep them warm.

The Lady sent Juan Diego to the bishop to show the bishop the flowers. After some difficulty, Juan Diego saw the bishop. When the bishop opened the cloak, the flowers fell to the floor and an image of the Lady remained on the cloak. A miraculous sign.

The bishop built a church at the place where the Lady appeared, as she requested. The entire event began a period of massive conversion and extended peace between the native Mexican Indians and the conquistador Spanish.

Despite its delicate fibers, the cloak has lasted. The image is still intact today and on display at the Shrine, over 490 years ago.

Today, people from all over the world visit the Shrine and ask for Mary's prayers and help for every type of living situation. Mary gave a message of hope to Juan Diego. That message applies to you, too.

Mary is the patroness of unborn children, and mother to you and your family.

The Song's History

In August 1997, I promised to write a song for the Hispanic community of our Catholic Church parish, the Church of the Holy Spirit in Schaumburg, IL. They were celebrating the Banquetes de las Rosas (The Banquet of Roses) that November.

On September 25, 1997, the inspiration for the song came as I was praying. I wrote the lyrics and later that day, composed the melody, and created the sheet music. I sang the song at the banquet and recorded it at a sound studio.

On December 12, 1997, I received the cassette tapes of that song. On March 1, 1998, my wife and I made a pilgrimage to the Basilica of Our Lady of Guadalupe in Mexico City.

We had been married for 15 years and did not have any pregnancies. We went to the Shrine to pray for a conception and a baby. On April 2, we discovered we were pregnant. On December 3, 1998, our beautiful daughter was born. We are so very grateful for this wonderful blessing.

Treasuring Lyrics

In one cold winter, when snow was falling, there came a lady, whose voice was calling. She chose a poor one to spread her message, a gift of flowers, blossoms of hope.

She gave him roses, petals from heaven sprouted from her love, grown in her heart. She brings us roses, sign of protection, clothed in her promise of lasting prayer.

Refrain
O blessed Virgin, make us a garden, plant in us God's word, that Jesus may reign. Santa Maria, pray for the Spirit, gather your harvest, de las rosas de mi.

We share God's roses as we hold each hand, so sweet the fragrance, so tender to touch. We are God's roses, bouquet of Mary, given to Jesus, held by God's heart.
Refrain

In night of winter, blossoms are sleeping, the poor are crying, for justice weeping. We must bring roses to ease their burden, Santa Maria: we answer your prayer.
Refrain

Scan the QR code to play the song:

The Song's Meaning

Las Rosas de Maria is a song of hope. The first two verses of the song tell the story of Our Lady of Guadalupe and her message to Juan Diego in December 1531. The Blessed Virgin Mary promised her protection and prayers to all people. Her prayers are with each of us today–all we need to do is ask.

The refrain asks the prayers of Mary to make us a garden of God's word, so that Jesus may be the king of our hearts. We ask Mary, who conceived Jesus by the power of the Holy Spirit, to ask the Spirit to conceive Jesus in our thoughts, words, and actions. We ask Mary to gather the harvest of "my roses"–the good that we do for others.

The third verse is an identity verse about us. We are God's roses. God created each person with majestic beauty and a sweet fragrance. We belong to one another, like a bouquet of roses. Mary gives that bouquet to Jesus, and is held by God's heart.

The fourth verse is about God's call to make things good and right in our lives and in the lives of others. The "night of winter" and "blossoms are sleeping" refers to the dark and troubling times that many people live in today.

The poor are crying for help–for justice weeping. Your unborn child is poor. He cries to get your attention and love. She needs your love through your positive emotions, treasuring words and songs, food and oxygen through your bloodstream, shelter in your partner's womb, and a safe home and family after birth.

During pregnancy, your call is to ease your unborn child's burden by bringing roses: words and acts of love and kindness. You are the Juan Diego to your family. God wants to build a temple in your lives and in your home. You are temples of the Holy Spirit. As a spiritual mom to you and your family, Mary's prayers are with you today and always.

Related Books

Scan the QR code to purchase the books online.

For Expecting Dads

A Concert from Mary and Joseph to Expecting Dads

A Retreat with Mary and Joseph for Expecting Dads

For Expecting Moms

Singing Treasuring Songs to Your Unborn Child

Mary's Love Songs for Expecting Moms

www.ingramcontent.com/pod-product-compliance
Lightning Source LLC
LaVergne TN
LVHW041109080826
845145LV00007B/1742
9781963227598